Faith to Practice
Foundations of Happiness

David Gaia Kano

ISBN-13: 978-1976274299
ISBN-10: 197627429X

Dedication

This book is dedicated to all the
spiritual seekers in the world. May their practice benefit all
beings and bring peace.

Table of Contents

Acknowledgements

Many people influenced and contributed to the content of this book and, perhaps more important, supported me in my spiritual practices. I want to give thanks to my late mother, whose last gift inspired me to start a practice of non-judgment; to my daughters, who never complained when it was time for me to go off to meditate; to my sister Susan, my closest spiritual confidant and emergency contact, who has also read all of Dr. David Hawkins's books and has helped me to understand his teachings; to my friends in the York family, especially Andrea and John, for encouraging me to go with them to the Transcendental Meditation introductory lecture back in 1972; to Gendo Allyn Field at the Upper Valley Zen Center, for providing a disciplined approach for my first significant experience in group meditation; to all the facilitators and regular attenders at the Heart of the Valley Mindfulness Practice Center, who first inspired me to start a mindfulness practice during life's little chores; to the folks at the Center for Transformational Practice, for providing a rich environment for practice and reflection that led to the first version of the creed I share herein; to Mark Kutolowski, who inspired me to adopt beliefs from my Christian roots

i

with an emphasis on contemplation and Divine Unity; to the folks at Koinonia Farm, who continued my Christian education and provided rich opportunities for spiritual study and practice; to Betsy Alexander and Laurel Stavis for their fine editing; to Jen Kano for the beautiful cover design and photos, and to my friend Karl Rosengrant, for allowing me to help him start a new eco-village which is now my wonderful home and haven for practice.

Introduction

Perhaps the most important thing I've learned, since I started meditating twice a day in 1972, is that happiness is 95% interpretation and 5% circumstances. Modern assumptions about happiness, which are even alluded to in the U.S. Declaration of Independence, are that we must "pursue" happiness through material wealth, fame, and other circumstances external to ourselves. As I've matured spiritually, I've found a source of happiness that is independent of my economic and even social situations. My faith-based beliefs have been the source of inspiration, spiritual energy and devotion that have made that independence possible, through practice.

While I wrote this book, I re-read many of the books I've found useful in my own spiritual journey. I wanted to see how they addressed the ideas I was seeking to convey. What I found over and over was a bit surprising, even though I'd read and enjoyed these books for years, some of them many times. The ideas that people had to "take on faith" (with no supporting proof or explanations) were interspersed with other ideas, sometimes with little regard to their interdependence and usually with no mention of the need to have faith. The authors were leaving it up to their readers to decide which ideas are based on faith. As one wrote, "Take what resonates, and leave the rest."

It is important to recognize and honor foundational beliefs that require faith. Many of the ideas that I have adopted, and daily practices they engender, are upheld by my faith. They follow or depend on each other. When I have trouble, when I find myself wavering in the process of making an important life decision, I look to my faith for strength and guidance. I try to get back to my most fundamental beliefs, upon which all others rest. If I did not know what those fundamentals were, I'd be lost. It would be like navigating a challenging journey without a map and compass, like trying to love without a heart.

Discovering what we currently believe facilitates the journey of shaping our faith so that it supports life practices that will lead to happiness and success. Because it is never too late to say, "I believe," in something new!

About the Author

If you are still discerning whether or not to read this book, or invite me to speak to your community group, you may want to know more about me. From where did I come to my opinions on faith and practice? While I've cited some reputable sources for the ideas that I've learned (intellectually) from others, the main ideas in this book have (also) been realized as true through spiritual insight. This is a kind of heartfelt certainty of belief, that itself is also what I'd call "faith." These insights have come in the context of decades of regular daily spiritual practice, as detailed below.

I don't usually like to "blow my own horn," especially when it comes to my spiritual practices and signs of "progress." I'm just a humble college drop-out, who understands that the danger of "spiritual pride" is that it can be a seeker's downfall. Pride can quite literally come before the fall, as the expression goes.

Despite this concern, I've opened myself to share deeply about my practices and experiences, with the hope that they will inspire you to seek (to strengthen) your own faith-based beliefs to better support your own (more regular) life-supporting practices. I'd like to be part of that support system, through this book and, for some of you, through face-to-face teaching opportunities. For that, you will need to have some faith in me!

I was born March 8, 1957 in Boston, Massachusetts and raised in the Episcopal Church, by virtue of being the grandson of an Episcopal priest. My father took us to church most Sundays and insisted that I go to confirmation class when I was 11 or 12, but I refused to be confirmed, as the Trinity had no meaning for me. I was agnostic for the first 27 years of my life.

When I started practicing Transcendental Meditation (TM) twice a day at age 15, it was mainly for the stress-relieving benefits. In Chapter 4 I share more about how I came to the practice of TM.

At 27 years old, I adopted faith in God as Love while attending Quaker meeting in Cambridge, Massachusetts. I share more about this in Chapter 5.

When I was 31, I broke and dislocated my neck. I was having a manic episode, though I did not realize and admit to that until decades later. As I was being flown from a small local hospital to a regional teaching hospital for surgery, I affirmed in prayer, "Dear God, I love the world and all the people in it so much! If I can walk and move my arms again, I'll be better able to spend the rest of my life giving to others." The surgery went well and I've been trying to fulfill that promise ever since, in one way or another.

I married at age 34, and in the subsequent years my wife and I raised two girls, now both wonderful young women. My wife and I separated in 2001 and subsequently divorced, sharing equal custody of the girls. In the process of separation I changed my last name from Munsey-Kano back to Kano, adding the middle name "Gaia" because of my belief in global unity. I share more about this in Chapter 5.

Not long before my mother died, when I was 39, she gave me a final gift: a copy of the book *The Seven Spiritual Laws of Success* by Deepak Chopra. This book inspired me to start a practice of non-judgment, which I now prefer to call "Radical Acceptance." I describe this further in Chapter 4.

At age 43 I undertook Reiki training, and within two years was certified as a Reiki master/teacher. Reiki is a gentle energy healing modality.[1] I have given myself daily treatments ever since and often use Reiki during my silent meditations.

At 49 I quit drinking alcohol, in an experiment of total sobriety to support spiritual growth and mindfulness. This experiment eventually became a lifelong commitment.

When my children were young we lived in West Lebanon, New Hampshire and attended the Unitarian Universalist Church of the Upper Valley. When I was 53, I left looking for a more theist church, but not finding one that was compatible with my beliefs, I ended up at the Upper Valley Zen Center (UVZC) in White River

---

[1] For more information, please visit www.reiki.org.

Junction, Vermont. The attraction of UVZC was that silent practice has no content that I felt needed "translation," as was the case in the Christian churches; these placed too little emphasis on Divine Unity for my taste. This was my first experience of a significant amount of group meditation practice, after 38 years of meditating twice a day at home.

Turning 55 was a big year for me in many ways. In December I finally retired from my computer programming career, which I had enjoyed at 25, but which I had come to find lacking in opportunities to "make a real difference" meaningful to others.

Spiritual practice had become more important to me than ever. In March, I started an experiment in celibacy. I decided not to look for a new primary relationship, because the transitional nature of my life was likely to take me out of the Upper Valley area. Shortly thereafter I experienced a mini awakening.

I started to experience the radiant beauty of all of creation, which later inspired me to write these poems:

Illuminating Now

A thing is beautiful
when it inspires
attention
to hold you fully,
and profoundly,
in this moment.

Conversely...

When you dare
to live purely
in the naked now,
  diligently,
    gently,
      patiently releasing the veils
of judgment,
  interpretation,
    comparison
      and memory,

you will experience
a radiant beauty
with all of creation!

Contrast

Radical commitment
    to practice
    acceptance
illuminates
everything.

Experience
radiant perfection
in shimmering edges
of cumulous clouds,
backlit by the sun;
in silhouettes of trees
at dusk,
against the gentle sky;

in side-lit textures
of walls and ceilings,
mere bumps of paint.

Be contrast between
    light and dark,
    joy and pain,
    compassion and judgment
Be sublime textures of
    perception,
    thought,
    feeling.
Be full spectrum equanimity
    laughing annoyance,
    inspirational pain,
    serious joy.
Be gentle arms of compassion
    accept attachments
    embrace suffering.

When you're ready,
surrender!

This perception lasted steadily for three months or so. After it faded, it could be restored again through extended meditation practice, such as a 1-2 day solo retreat. I didn't mind so much when this perception was not with me, because I knew that perfection of creation is still the reality in which we live; I was just not able to see it all the time yet. The experience strengthened my devotion to spiritual practice.

In the middle of that same year, I started to practice meditation at the Heart of the Valley Mindfulness Practice

Center, whose members mainly follow the Buddhist teachings of Thich Nhat Hanh and the Plum Village Monastery he founded. Inspired by his teachings, I started to practice mindfulness meditation during repetitive tasks like washing dishes, routine walking (e.g. to refill my water glass at work) and more. Over the course of the next 2-3 years, this practice would become continuous throughout every day as I made the transition to being a full time contemplative practitioner.

For years I'd wanted to live in an intentional community of some kind, and began a search for same. I looked into becoming a monk, but all of the monasteries I found had age requirements: I was too old to be considered.

When I was 57 I went to a Buddhist retreat where I received the five mindfulness trainings and was given the dharma name "Virtuous Friend of the Source" by Michael Ciborsky, a former monk at Plum Village. The five mindfulness trainings are a modern form of Buddhist rules to live by, to support practice and live a wholesome, loving life.[2]

I spent the year that I turned 58 (2015) as an intern at Koinonia Farm in Americus, Georgia —a Christian "new monastic" intentional community established in 1942—. This was another very big year for my practice. In March I started a full time practice of staying with the sense "I am" as taught by Sri Nisargardatta Maharaj in his book *I Am That*. I share more about this practice and the beliefs that

---

[2] See https://plumvillage.org/mindfulness-practice/the-5-mindfulness-trainings/ (accessed 9/4/17).

support it in Chapter 5. In October of that year I experienced another awakening.

I started to experience ubiquitous love of everything and everyone, a.k.a. bliss, throughout every day. This was first realized during a morning meditation when I experienced the heartfelt thought, "Every moment is a precious opportunity to explore who and what I am." I had fallen in love with the "I am" practice of releasing most thoughts as they arose throughout the day. The energy of my earnest devotion had increased and with it came the experience of Divine love, a.k.a. presence of God. As I moved throughout my day, I had the warm feeling of "being in love" but without the attachment that had always come with my previous experiences of romantic love. Wherever I cast my gaze, there was the object of my love, in all of its perfect beauty. My experience of other people was even more sublime. Everyone was perfectly lovable and radiantly beautiful. I found myself entranced by this realization, as I feasted on the presence of God in everyone with whom I worked and met at the farm. Through this experience I realized for myself the teaching of Nisargardatta, that bliss is actually our natural state, we just cover it up with our habits of mind including judgments, preferences, fears and desires. I'd come home to myself, though I knew that I'd not yet reached the full fruition of Enlightenment.

By the end of December the state of bliss had subsided, as I made plans to leave Koinonia and travel back to the Upper Valley. My life had, however, been changed for good. It was clearer than ever to me that continuous spiritual practice would always be the most important thing, and that I needed to find a living situation that would support that priority.

On my return to the Upper Valley in 2016, I decided to help my friend Karl Rosengrant start a small Eco-village in South Royalton, Vermont. An important factor in that decision was my desire to settle back into devoted practice without all the distractions of discernment and travel that would have been required to continue searching for other pre-existing community options. I'd experienced the reality that the details of my situation were unimportant, other than being settled enough to practice "I am" with minimal distractions. In April, even before I could start to get set up to live on that land, from time to time I regained the experience of ubiquitous radiant beauty and bliss, as I had at Koinonia. Continuing the "I am" practice, while simply knowing the direction that my residential life was going, was quite fruitful. I spent the year setting up camp and then building an off-grid tiny house in which I now live, all the while making spiritual practice my foundational, primary goal.

I'm writing this in 2017, the year I turned 60. In March, I changed the "experimental" status of my celibacy to a lifelong commitment, and held a ceremony at the Center for Transformational Practice in White River Junction, Vermont,[3] to affirm that decision among supportive friends. Shortly thereafter, the experience of unconditional Love for everything (bliss) returned more steadily, in

---

[3]   http://transformationalpractice.org/

conjunction with seitai[4] massage treatments from Eliza Meeker.

For the next 2-3 months, I experienced dozens of episodes where the blissful feeling of Love was so overpowering that the ego broke down into tears of ecstasy and gratitude. At times it seemed unbelievable that I could "deserve" the state that I had reached, because it was so sweetly Divine. This was particularly true during one of the seitai treatments with Eliza, which inspired this poem:

Deal of a Lifetime

Meditating twice a day,
for 45 years.
Practicing radical acceptance,
for 21 years.
11 years of sobriety.
5 years of nearly
full time mindfulness
and chastity.
Practicing the sense,
"I am" nearly
full time for 2 years.
All of it done for its own sake,
the process
is the goal.
With no attachment to possible outcomes

---

[4]   Seitai is a deep tissue massage and energy healing modality that Eliza learned when she lived in Japan for 10 years.

of shifting consciousness
to higher planes.
It's the process
that is shifting,
fed by the fruits of devotion,
which come to inspire
earnest
practice,
in a positive feedback loop,
that's a true blessing.

Ubiquitous radiant beauty,
holds me in each moment,
automatic mindfulness.
While blissfully Loving everything,
old habits of the fearful mind
are whispers,
easy to release.
Moments of ecstasy,
with overwhelming gratitude
for the presence of God.
Each moment
is a precious
opportunity,
to explore
"I am."

45 minutes into another sweetly painful,
seitai,
deep tissue massage.
Energy throbbing
down both arms,
became smooth
and strong enough,

to cradle God,
for a full ten minutes of Ecstasy.
Divine tears of welcome,
poured
from my eyes.
With sobs of gratitude,
and whimpers of humility.
Indescribable.

Crying too hard
to speak at first,
I managed to whimper "joy,"
and then a croak of "grateful."
Hopefully my healer
would kind of understand.
Overwhelmed
through it All
I humbly tried to convey,
"I have no
idea
how I
deserve
to be having
this experience!"
I thought, "How is this happening,
to tiny little me?
What did I ever do
to deserve
this?"
My lifetime
of practice,
couldn't
measure up.

As the tears subsided
she asked, "Are you okay,
do you need anything?"
The feeling of perfect completeness
brought a long
hearty laugh.
"Please don't be offended by my laughter."
"I'm not offended, but what are you laughing about?"
Still laughing, I replied, "It's impossible."
"What's impossible?"
"To need anything!"

These ecstatic episodes lasted anywhere from a few seconds to several minutes, and seemed often to be triggered by seeing something that I would have appreciated as beautiful before I had realized the radiant beauty of everything. It was as if the combination of the higher awareness of ubiquitous love and beauty along with the ego's estimation of beauty was too much to take in without a very energetic emotional response. These ecstatic moments were something like a spiritual orgasm, at least ten times more intense than any sexual experience. Naturally I started to look for when the next one would come, yet I knew from studying the writings of David Hawkins in his book *Transcending the Levels of Consciousness: The Stairway to Enlightenment* that even this would have to be surrendered to God in order to continue my journey.

In April, I had the insight that I was ready to start that process of release. The ecstatic reactions to my state of bliss were just another ego-based experience, which stood in the path of spiritual "progress." Whenever the feeling of ecstasy started to rise, I breathed through it as I surrendered it to God. During one of these moments, while riding my motorcycle to White River Junction one foggy morning, I was inspired to write this Haiku:

> When ecstasy comes
> I let it pass over me
> Like sun above fog

After a month or two of this process, I rarely broke down into ecstatic tears anymore, and I'd found a new level of peace in the blissful process.

In June, during another seitai massage treatment, I found the "I am the witness" state that Nisargardatta often mentions in his teachings. As the witness only, I shifted to an awareness of the deep tissue work as a mere pressure, even on muscles which were so tight that I'd been experiencing the pressure as excruciatingly painful only moments before. This was a state of deep peace, where my heart and breath actually slowed to the steady states of a sitting meditation session, even as the deep tissue massage continued. In a subsequent session a couple of weeks later, I was able to reach that state of witnessing by meditating on it for 5-10 minutes before the treatment started, so that even the initial deep muscle work was not experienced as painful.

My life to date has been such a blessing in so many ways. Even before I started to see these previews of the ultimate awakening, I was very grateful for the abundance of wonderful opportunities, loving relationships, experiences and material blessings I had. Ever since I broke and dislocated my neck in 1988, I've wanted to give the love that I'd found back to the world. I've done my best to make good on the promise that I prayed that day.

Now that I've experienced the peaceful presence of God through my practices, I feel called to finally finish this book and get out into the world to find others who are ready to make wholesome practices such as mindfulness meditation a part of their daily lives. Because the best gift I can think of is the inspiration to explore one's own consciousness and, with the grace of God, return to one's naturally   blissful   state.

1 Your Life Rests on Faith

What do we want from life: health, happiness, love, security, peace of mind, spiritual growth? This book offers some ideas that can help us, through practice, build the kinds of lives we want to live and become the people we want to be.

Our beliefs are very important. They guide the choices, at least the conscious ones, that shape our lives. Yet many people leave to chance the determination of what they believe. They spend little time thinking about and really understanding their foundational beliefs. These are taken for granted as a given, presumably unchangeable, part of who we are. If you don't change your beliefs, and/or start doing a better job of living through them, you will keep making the same choices.

We have all heard the benefits of various life practices and healing processes that we can use to improve our health and happiness: meditation, prayer, compassion, mindfulness, forgiveness, tolerance, loving our neighbor, generosity, getting enough sleep, exercise, taking time to relax and recreate, spending quality time with our children or loved ones, and many more. For many of us, we are doing better than usual if we can point to one instance per day of doing even one of these time-proven practices. Why is this? We lack faith. Our primary beliefs and assumptions allow and support, if not inspire, other behaviors and priorities. These behaviors often become habits that are hard to change, even after we have adopted beliefs with which they are inconsistent.

If we want to change our lives for the better, by taking more actions that will (for example) strengthen our loving relationships, increase our gratitude and help us find inner peace and happiness, we need beliefs that will support and inspire us to keep regular practices that will improve the qualities of our lives. We need to stop taking our belief systems for granted as a "given," unchangeable aspect of ourselves, as I did too, when I was young.

For the first 27 years of my life, I was agnostic. I thought I did not have faith in anything, but was open to everything. My father is a mechanical engineer, and when I was a boy we spent many hours in the basement building things. In the process, he taught me some basic Newtonian physics, structural engineering, properties of electricity and more. We saw the world through materialist assumptions, some of which we understood as proven scientific facts.

When I allowed myself to ponder the meaning of life, the best I could come up with was that I was here to have fun. So we built mini-bikes, a short wave radio, unicycles, a sailing land yacht and more. The most fun I'd found was in the thrill of riding a vehicle faster, over new terrain, with the resulting feeling of power, control and acceleration. None of this required me to have faith in anything, or so I thought.

What is faith? One definition is, "firm belief in something for which there is no proof." You may know people who claim, by this definition, not to have "faith" in anything. They need scientific proof to believe. To them, "facts" are fundamental, while "faith" is only considered in the context of formal religious or spiritual life, which are held separate from their day-to-day routines. This is certainly how I felt in my youth. I thought faith-based beliefs were optional.

I'd like to offer a different definition of faith as "a foundational belief, upon which all your other beliefs depend." By this definition, we all have faith. The question is, faith in what? In his book *Discovering the Presence of God*, Dr. David Hawkins says:

> All people live by faith. The only variable is in 'what' that faith is placed. The selection reflects a level of consciousness that, in turn, is correlated with perception, values, and intrinsic capacity for comprehension and primary motivation.[5]

Hawkins believes that the faith we "choose" tends to change with our stage of spiritual development or "level of consciousness." I agree, but I also believe that from time to time our consciousness rises above our norm, providing opportunities for us to perceive and adopt

---

[5] Dr. David Hawkins, Discovery the Presence of God, (Veritas Publishing 2006) p. 47, Kindle edition location 550.

beliefs that are more supportive of fruitful life practices. I'll explore this idea further in Chapter 5, "Faithful Evolution."

Our life is like a house. We want it to be a pleasant place to live, to meet all our needs. Unlike our physical home, our life sits on a foundation of faith. Our faith-based beliefs lead to other beliefs which lead to actions. These actions help to create our life. Our beliefs also determine how we interpret our circumstances and challenges. Many people who have a strong faith in God understand this concept through their faith. For example, they may see everything in relationship to "God's will" or "God's plan" for them. Let's explore how even people who are not "spiritual" or religious depend on their faith-based beliefs.

We know if we throw a rock into the air, it is eventually going to fall back down. Newton's law applies. The Earth spins on its axis, which causes day and night. People are born and they die (at least physically). These are the "facts of life" but they, too, sit on a foundation of faith—faith in science, repeatability, and the scientific method—and at the root of all that, faith that the information we receive from our senses is real. Without faith in the evidence of our senses, we cannot prove anything.

In the popular movie *The Matrix*, a future earth has been taken over by machines, which use human beings as their source of energy. Most of the humans exist at the physical level in a bath of water, being fed intravenously, their energy being drawn out by some fantastic high-tech method, to drive the machines that rule the world. In spite of this, the people think they are living normal lives in a world like ours. Their minds are linked to a massive computer program that simulates their entire world. Everything they experience is coming through fiber optic strands in the back of their necks.

Of course this is science fiction, but the point is, we really can't be sure. Each of us could, in fact (to give another example) be nothing more than a small part of a virtual reality computer program, designed by an intelligent being. We would not need "real" physical bodies at all, just the ability to process the information fed to our subroutine selves, plus some kind of artificial intelligence to allow us to learn and evolve "mentally." Most people will not give this notion a second thought as they continue to read. We "know" better, even though there is no way to prove otherwise. We have faith in our own reality.

We have faith in our senses. Most people have faith in science to tell us what is repeatable and therefore "true." We are human beings. We live on Earth, a planet orbiting the sun, which is one of billions of stars in our galaxy. A scientist will tell you that everything we "know" rests upon what we already held to be true. At times science makes a breakthrough: we find out something we didn't know before, and what had been seen as "facts" become marginalized or even outright falsehoods. Even in science, what is believed to be true can evolve.

This book is about evaluating and evolving our faith foundations, so we can make joyful choices that help to support a joyful life. The first chapters are a general exploration of this concept of faith, with some examples of common beliefs and their influence. Chapter 4 contains a snapshot, from 2012, of my personal creed and practices that it supports. This creed is drawn from a combination of Buddhist, Christian, and scientific sources. The final chapters of the book outline a process that will help us explore and transform our faith-based beliefs, so they will support positive, life-changing practices.

As Hawkins notes, our chosen faith is at least somewhat dependent on where we are in our spiritual journeys. A person for whom life is pure misery will not believe in a God of pure love. A joyful person who sees the Divine beauty in all of creation cannot fathom a judgmental God who would condemn a soul to eternal damnation. People come to their faith often through some life-changing event. In the process of their transformation, they see God in a new light. In that respect, perhaps it is academic to discuss the process of choosing your faith, but I believe within each of our current limitations there are still choices. We can choose a faith foundation that helps us to stretch and grow. We can examine our beliefs and find some we are ready to release, which no longer support us well. We can rediscover what we already believe and commit ourselves to living by our "highest faith" when mindfully making our everyday life choices.

Everyone is a choice-maker. we choose what and whom to believe, and many of those choices depend at some level on faith: faith in our parents, our teacher, pastor, rabbi or other spiritual leader; faith that authorities in our lives are speaking truths to live by. We can call this trust if we like, but underlying that trust is faith.

The beliefs that are most important to our happiness go beyond our physical worlds. They affect our relationships, expectations, judgments, attitudes and interpretations, and can make the difference between happiness and misery. They make the difference between committing to a daily spiritual practice, and going to church only on religious holidays—between creating a life we love or one we merely endure.

2   Examples of Beliefs
and
What They Support

This book will help us look at our faith foundations, and decide whether they are supporting the life we want to live. Most of us rely on beliefs that do exactly the opposite. Let's look at some examples.

"Murphy's Law" says, more or less, that if something can go wrong, it will. To demonstrate how often this belief is affirmed, listen for the words "of course" in everyday conversations. "We got to the movies close to starting time, so of course the one we wanted to see was sold out." Or, "There's been lots of rain in the forecast, but it's been pretty nice all week. I left my umbrella at home for the first time today, so of course it was pouring when I got out of work!"

This is a self-fulfilling prophesy. When we subscribe to Murphy's Law, we notice when things go wrong and reinforce them with expressions of exasperation. We remind ourselves that the world is out to get us, by emphasizing and making mention of the bad more frequently than the good. That last example could have been "Boy, we were lucky not to get as much rain this week as was predicted. I really appreciated that today, when I got soaked running to my car!" Even though this practice is prevalent in our culture, it's useful to remind ourselves that "Murphy was not a lawyer, he was a liar!

Murphy's Law is an example of a belief or assumption that we can change. In order to replace it with belief in abundance, we may need to change some of our faith foundations, because a belief well-supported by faith is more likely to endure.

Consumer Culture

Another common belief has to do with happiness and success. We are constantly exposed to advertisements that try to convince us, often successfully, that we need certain products to enhance our lives. These things will make us look stylish and desirable, save us time, keep us safe or entertained, etc. The advertisements tell us that we're unhappy with what we have and urge us to try for happiness by buying more. The mind is easily fooled and the ego loves a conflict, so these pervasive messages are convincing billions of people they are miserable. Even the wealthy fall victim to this folly.

Most of us have experienced this. We get excited about something new, save our money and buy it. At first the new thing really is great and it seems to make us happy, but eventually the excitement wanes and that thing starts to blend into the scenery of life. We need something new to be excited about, and spending money on the new thing just continues the cycle.

The best defense against this pervasive belief is to realize our inner source of happiness. Fundamental qualities such as acceptance, gratitude, generosity, forgiveness, peace of mind, and love are the stuff of enduring happiness. If we really believe that, we will be inspired to work at strengthening these qualities in ourselves. In Chapter 4 we'll consider some time-proven spiritual practices that can help us realize true happiness within.

Materialistic Assumptions

Our culture is in love with science and technology. We love our cell phones, computers, microwaves and many other conveniences. The acceptance of science is so prevalent that most of us don't see this as an area of faith. Science is quite good at helping us make decisions about the physical world, but in other areas science falls short.

Most scientists rely on the assumption that everything can be explained in terms of mechanical / chemical / atomic actions and reactions, forces and counter forces that can be observed, measured and recorded. But their faith in materialism is open to question. Rupert Sheldrake has written extensively on the limitations of this faith in science. For example, in his book *Science Set Free* he discusses the common assumption that our memories are physically stored in our brains. This assumption is unproven; in fact there is evidence to the contrary which, however, most neurologists refute out-of-hand. The usefulness of science is severely limited by this blind faith in materialism. For example, scientists rarely study alternative modalities of healing. Even when they undertake such studies, researchers have difficulty finding collaborators in the scientific community who will test their findings. Scientific journals often dismiss such research as quackery, because it falls outside of science's materialistic assumptions.

Our faith in science lets us rely on gravity, understand our need for clean air, consider our response to climate change, and so on. Many scientific concepts are an important part of our daily lives and understanding them can help us with our relationship to the physical world. Fundamentally, science teaches us is that our universe is not random, but is governed by laws. But in spite of science's great value to us, we must understand its limitations.

Our world is also governed by spiritual laws, for example the law of karma, which basically says we reap what we sow. These spiritual laws are no less real than the law of gravity. And just as our belief in scientific laws rests on our faith in science, our belief in spiritual laws also must rest on faith in order to serve as foundation for our lives.

Verbally Affirming Our Beliefs

Language is powerful. When we employ words and phrases carelessly, we can unwittingly do harm by reinforcing their actual meaning. When that literal meaning describes an undesirable process or belief we tend to increase our suffering. My late mother, bless her soul, used to say "You need to worry about _____!" Fill in the blank with anything that was happening or could happen in the future that required action. At one point I actually challenged her and said, "No mom, I don't. I need to plan and prepare for that, and I am." It may sound like nit-picking, but I really think our words reflect our realities even when they are not intended to be literally true. My mom sure knew how to worry!

In another example, many people use a phrase like, "You made me feel bad (sad, angry, happy) when you said (did) that." The undesirable literal meaning is that others have the power to control our feelings. We are saying, even if we don't believe it, that others are responsible for our feelings, that they need to take care in what they do and say around us lest they force us to suffer difficult feelings! A more accurate way to articulate these situations is through "I messages" such as "When you said (did) that, I felt bad (sad, angry, happy)." Even better, we could explain why we felt that way, to try to be better understood.

These examples show how our (sometimes unconscious) beliefs or behaviors can creep into our language, which then reinforces them. We may say, accurately, that we're worried about something we're preparing to do, but do we really want to let our language reinforce worry? We may feel a negative response to words that others use, but we don't have to let this feeling control us. Yet these words can creep into our own language, reinforcing their negative effect. Using the exasperated phrase "of course" before recounting a negative experience reinforces our belief that we are victims.

Patient mindfulness can help us mold more beneficial beliefs. We can eliminate language that reinforces beliefs that cause suffering, being gentle with ourselves in this process. Changing negative habits can take time.

3 Habits and Addictions

We all do some things out of habit. Some are helpful, like always putting the car keys in the same place so they can be easily found. Some are not so helpful, like chewing our fingernails or turning on the TV even when there's nothing on that interests us. This is not a book about breaking habits or recovering from addiction, but it would be naive to ignore these challenges as we try to make choices that change our lives for the better. It can be a difficult process to consciously apply our beliefs to our choices, and there are other barriers that often need to be addressed.

This chapter will give a brief overview of some common habits and some resources for breaking them. I will also highlight how we are all addicted to one or more behaviors and/or things. Addiction doesn't always stand in our way as we try to live happier lives. Some addictions may actually be helpful, such as spiritual practices.

It can be helpful to simply recognize that we do some things out of habit. This is one motivation for being more mindful. Perhaps a mindfulness practice is needed to successfully start any new practice. If this sounds like a

"Catch-22," welcome to the paradoxical world of spiritual wisdom!

The most difficult habits to break are ones that come with a reward. Because our bodies can become addicted to the neuropeptides secreted when we have an emotion, many of our habits are rewarded. Neuropeptides are chemicals secreted by glands to send messages throughout our brains and bodies. The process of addiction to them is described by Candice Pert and some of the other scientists in the movie *What the Bleep Do We Know!?*[6] Every cell in our bodies has receptors for these neuropeptides, and habitual behavior builds our need for them. When we habitually experience an emotion, our bodies actually go into withdrawal if we go too long without that emotion. Then we (often subconsciously) do something to experience it again and get our "fix."

For example, let's say we are in the habit of complaining. Murphy's Law seems to be in full force in our lives, and we love to get together with friends to discuss our misfortunes. We could very well be addicted to sorrow, or to scorn if we blame our problems on others. If we often feel we are victims of uncontrollable circumstances, we are probably addicted to the neuropeptides secreted by these feelings. Fortunately, they

---

6 "What the Bleep Do We Know!? is a 2004 film that combines documentary-style interviews, computer-animated graphics, and a narrative that posits a spiritual connection between quantum physics and consciousness."
(https://en.wikipedia.org/wiki/What_the_Bleep_Do_We_Know!%3F, accessed 8/15/17).

can be short-circuited by recognition and will power. It is also helpful to ask friends and family members to remind us to stop when we get started with our habitual behavior! I know this from experience.

When she was young, my daughter Rose used to have a lot of small accidents. She would come to me a couple of times a week with a stubbed toe or finger, a scrape or bump. I'd ask her where it hurt, check to see if it needed first aid, and say, "I'm sorry you hurt yourself. I think it will feel better soon, it doesn't look too serious." After a good hug she would be off. Eventually, I noticed that this was a pattern and saw a connection to what I'd learned from Candice Pert in the movie mentioned earlier. I wasn't sure my daughter was addicted to sorrow, but I shared with her the basic mechanisms involved and she seemed to appreciate the possibility. The next time she came to me looking for sympathy, I smiled and asked, "Do you think you might be here for a 'sorrow fix'?" As her eyes and mouth opened wide, she turned on her heel and left before I even examined her injury!

Eventually, she stopped coming to me with little boo-boos. I'm not sure if she stopped having the little accidents right away, or if she just stopped coming for sympathy until they ceased. Either way, I'm confident she "kicked the habit"!

I believe Rose originally became addicted to sorrow when I separated from her mother several years earlier. Her mother and I were both very sorry that she only had easy access to one of her parents at a time. She would come to one of us, missing the other, and we would tell her we were sorry. When she got older, she didn't miss her other parent as much or as often, but she still needed a reason to feel sorrow after the original cause was reduced. When she became aware that this was a habit, she was able to release it.

Our beliefs often motivate us to get started with a behavior that can become such a strong habit that it's hard to stop even when we change our beliefs. For example, we sincerely believe that we need a (certain) new possession to make us happy, so we go shopping. The anticipation of happiness while shopping and the initial pride and joy of ownership reinforces this belief. Then, at some point, we realize that our house is full of things we no longer use and they become a burden. We realize that the happiness we feel from our possessions doesn't last as long as the objects of our desire. Yet we still crave the feeling of excitement and anticipation we get while shopping and return to the store or website with no specific purchase in mind. At this point, we have recognized the false belief that consumption is connected to happiness, but we have not yet changed our behavior.

The Vietnamese Buddhist teacher Thich Nhat Hanh uses the term "habit energies" to describe the root of this problem. In *Understanding Our Mind* he writes:

> Because of habit energies, we are not able to perceive things as they truly are. We interpret everything we see or hear in terms of our habit energy.

Later he writes:

> Even though we may have the best intention to transform ourselves, we will not be successful

unless we work on our habit energies. The easiest way to do this is with a 'Sangha', a group of people who practice mindfulness together.[7]

We can create our own Sanghas, even if they are just groups of two, to help us live through our faith and transform old habits into new ones. If we ask trusted friends and loved ones for help, we can share our (new) belief with them and the practices it inspires. We can let them know which habits we are trying to let go of and ask for their help. Most people will be honored to join with us in this kind of effort. They may even be inspired to look into their own lives as a result.

We need to find or create a support group or Sangha that are not themselves stuck in the habit energy we are trying to transform and heal. We would not ask a happy drunk to help us stop drinking alcohol! It could also be difficult to ask the friend or group we usually complain with to help us see the world with more gratitude and stop feeling like a victim. The effort to find people who share our faith will be greatly rewarded. Not that they have to believe everything we believe in every detail, it is the actions and practices we are adopting that they should appreciate and support.

---

[7] Thich Nhat Hanh, *Understanding Our Mind* (Parallax Press, 2006), pp. 49 and 50.

4 Personal Creed of Faith and Practice

While I would be honored if readers adopted some or all of my beliefs, that is not the purpose of this book. Learning about others' belief systems can be helpful in affirming and seeking our own. All beliefs have some value on our spiritual journey, even those that we may later deprecate or refute. Ideally, we grow and change enough for our personal creeds to require updates throughout our lives. This doesn't mean we should "shop" often for a new spiritual / religious community in which to practice / worship, but throughout our lives we may find that we emphasize different facets of our faith traditions and appreciate new interpretations of their scriptures and teachings.

The value of our beliefs stems from the life practices they inspire. As Jesus taught, "For as the body apart from the spirit is dead, so also faith apart from works is dead."[8] I believe that life practices that help raise our consciousness are the most important, so they figure prominently in my personal creed.

---

[8] James 2:26.

Each part of my creed ends with a primary intention to pursue practice related to and supported by that belief, and the intention of each practice is to raise consciousness. If we can strengthen our current beliefs or adopt new ones that support wholesome practices, that works, too. There are many practices that help raise our consciousness, that I have not chosen to pursue regularly, such as martial arts (especially with an excellent teacher), reading scripture (*lectio divina* or otherwise), and many more. Our regular practices are best supported by cherished beliefs, along with the spiritual will to follow them.

When reading my creed, we may add the words "I believe" before each numbered section or each sentence, except for the last sentence in each section, since that is the statement of practice which follows from my belief.

Words in uppercase like Love and Self indicate a unified, Divine aspect. Lowercase pronouns like "i" are used to connote the semi-individualized self / ego.

The creed is organized so that the fundamental and all-encompassing aspects come first. This makes it possible to shorten it, as appropriate, by omitting some of the last sections. Subsequent beliefs are thus consistent with previous ones. When unsure how to interpret a particular belief, it may be helpful to reference one or more of the first, more fundamental beliefs. In this hierarchy there are different levels of belief, and as we move down away from the most fundamental ones we bring in more of the ego's illusions of separateness. These may be needed in order to support our practices, since the ego is involved in discerning how we spend our time!

Personal Creed of Faith and Practice:

1. The universe is fundamentally, Pan-universally, Unified. Exchanges between diversified manifestations benefit All. i live through gifts of Love. i will gratefully receive and give abundantly.

2. The source of all manifestation is pure, energetic Pan-universal Consciousness. God is the perfectly Loving co-creative relationship between diversified manifestations, and the relationship between all manifestations and Pan-universal Consciousness. i devote my life to God.

3. i am one of countless spiritual beings which manifest repeatedly as part of living Earth. God willing, i will continue to reincarnate here until all earthly beings are free from suffering.

4. Fundamental qualities in the life of a diversified spiritual being, such as happiness, compassion, grace, insight, and love, reflect each being's level of consciousness. It is the nature of manifest consciousness to rise in time from shame to Enlightenment. Mindfulness meditation facilitates this process. i will practice silent sitting meditation at least twice a day.

5. i am superficially human. my actions co-create my world and sow the karmic seeds of what i will eventually reap. Each moment is a perfect response to our karma, which contains many opportunities to learn and grow in Love. When i

fail to love, i will cherish the opportunity to forgive and affirm my devotion to God.

6. my heart can feel the Loving mind of God. The process of discernment, through radical acceptance of everyone I meet and of all creation, helps to reveal actions which reduce suffering. i will follow my heart in a practice of grateful acceptance.

7. Raising my consciousness (see part 4) supports Love, peace and clarification of truth for others. This facilitates others' own process of raising consciousness, so manifest consciousness rises exponentially. my faith and practice supports this journey. i will live by this creed, updating it as I change and grow in Love.

In summary, the practices supported by my creed are gratitude, generosity, devotion to a Loving God, steadfast commitment to reduce suffering on planet earth across multiple lifetimes, silent sitting meditation at least twice a day, forgiveness, heart-felt discernment, radical acceptance, and faithfulness.

Creed Part 1: Fundamental Unity and Gifts of Love

We all have our own most cherished belief. Mine is in bold below:

> **The universe is fundamentally, Pan-universally, Unified.** Exchanges between diversified manifestations benefit All. i live through gifts of Love. i will gratefully receive and give abundantly.

The term "Pan-Universally" was inspired by the string theory of universe creation as described by the advanced quantum physicist John Hagelin, PhD. The theory posits that universes are being created all the time, thus ours may not be the only one. I believe that all universes are unified with each other and with their source. In the absence (so far) of technology that can prove Hagelin's theories, belief in them requires faith and/or trust in the insights of spiritual teachers.

Hagelin says, "The universe is fundamentally unified and superficially diversified."[9] He is talking about our physical and energetic realities, but I believe this is true spiritually as well. Contemplatives from all religious traditions arrive at this same truth: "We are all one."[10]

Much of my own poetry explores this concept, for example this haiku:

> Individual
> Is also a collective
> Part of another

We are fortunate to live in an era when science is starting to affirm spiritual beliefs that are thousands of years old. This relieves the need to see our spiritual beliefs as being in conflict with science, if we choose our beliefs carefully.

---

[9] John Hagelin, Ph.D. on the DVD Explore the Frontiers of Consciousness, Creativity and the Brain (Maharishi University of Management, 2006 www.mum.edu).

[10] Any clear and explicit emphasis of Unity that Jesus may have offered has been lost in time and/or translation, though it is evident if one looks for it carefully. A good example is from John 17:20-23," "I do not ask for these only, but also for those who will believe in me through their word, that they may all be one, just as you Father are in me, and I in you, that they also may be in us, so that the world may believe that you have sent me. The glory that you have given me, I have given them, that they may be one even as we are one, I in they and they in me, that they may become perfectly one, so that the world will know that you sent me and loved them even as you loved me."

"The universe is fundamentally, Pan-universally, Unified. **Exchanges between diversified manifestations benefit All.** i live through gifts of Love. i will gratefully receive and give abundantly."

A paradox: we can be both separate individuals and unified with All. It is up to our perception and interpretation to see the difference, and even our perception is supported by our faith.

Giving and receiving is a benefit to everyone and everything. This belief stems directly from my faith in Unity. When people give to each other, they are actually giving to the entire universe so that everyone benefits. Giving affirms our personal experience of compassion and generosity, so that we can simultaneously experience both the giving and the receiving of each gift. We affirm our connection to each other and our belief in Unity at the same time. This is why Jesus taught that to give is more blessed than to receive.

"The universe is fundamentally, Pan-universally, Unified. Exchanges between diversified manifestations benefit All. **i live through gifts of Love.** i will gratefully receive and give abundantly."

The bold sentence above helps us to relate Unity to our individual selves. For example, we breathe in oxygen given by green plants, then exhale carbon dioxide which the plants need. When we hold in our hearts such constant exchanges, we grow in gratitude and faith in our fundamental Unity. Life requires exchange between all the diversified parts. No species can live on its own. In fact, of the millions of living cells in our bodies, the majority have no human DNA, but belong to other microscopic species that live symbiotically within us.

Relating consciously to our world, including other spiritual beings, allows us to feel Unity as our true reality. This is especially true in terms of love: when we give love to ourselves and others, we perceive our Unity.

I believe we can love others only as we love ourselves. When Jesus spoke of loving your neighbor as yourself, he meant it not so much a rule to live by as a law of love, the way love works.

This law of love stems from our Unity. Our love is not allocated for *either* ourselves or others, but applies to both. Love knows no separation, because there is none. Thus we can see that Love is God and God is Love (covered in the next part of my creed). Love teaches us who we are: Unified with All.

Albert Einstein agreed:

> A human being is part of a whole, called by us the "Universe," a part limited in time and space. He experiences himself, his thoughts and feelings, as something separated from the rest—a kind of optical delusion of his consciousness. This delusion is a kind of prison for us, restricting us to our personal desires and to affection for a few persons nearest us. Our task must be to free ourselves from this prison by widening our circles

of compassion to embrace all living creatures and
the whole of nature in its beauty.[11]

In the context of this description, it's important to
distinguish between emotional love, which often entails
attachment and judgment, and the fundamental,
compassionate, perfect Love that is of God. It's also
important to understand that phenomena such as
understanding, forgiveness and generosity are also
embodiments of love. Thus:

"The universe is fundamentally, Pan-universally,
Unified. Exchanges between diversified
manifestations benefit All. i live through gifts of
Love. **i will gratefully receive and give
abundantly.**"

Gratitude and generosity are a beautiful couple.
Through these heart connections the acts of receiving and
giving, necessary for all life, become spiritual practices.
This most fundamental of my beliefs supports the most
fundamental, life-supporting practice. As Deepak Chopra
writes, "In fact, anything that is of value in life only
multiplies when it is given." He goes on to explain, "It is
the intention behind your giving and receiving that is the
most important thing."[12] Faith in Unity allows the
intention of every action to support All.

---

[11] Albert Einstein to Robert S. Marcus, of the World Jewish
Congress, dated February 12, 1950, EA 60-424.

[12] Deepak Chopra, *The Seven Spiritual Laws of Success: A Practical
Guide To the Fulfillment of Your Dreams* (New World Library,
1994), p. 18.

When Jesus taught us to "lay up our treasure in heaven,"[13] He meant we should trust God to provide everything we need, so that even though we give away everything we have to others, there will still always be enough for all. Jesus lived in the reality of constant, life-supporting flow throughout all of creation. "Treasure in heaven" can also be understood as "good karma" as we raise our energetic consciousness.

At the most fundamental level, Unity encompasses all physical and semi-individualized spiritual realities. Unity is our beginning and our end.

Although it can be hard to grasp the abstract concept of our spiritual selves being unified with All, we can approach it more easily by considering what we are not. This is one of those wonderful paradoxes: in order to understand that each of us is unified with everything, we start by trying to ferret out things that we are not:

We are not our bodies. We seem to have bodies, but it is best to think of them as borrowed, like hats that keep us warm, until we return them from whence they came. A strong identification with our body can lead to much anguish and suffering, but when we realize the limitations of this belief, faith in our spiritual nature can help us to accept and love our body **and** our true Self.

We are not our thoughts. Thinking is akin to seeing. In fact Buddhism teaches that the mind is the sixth sensing organ. Thoughts come to us, we do not create them. They are not even uniquely "ours." It may be helpful to think of

---

[13] Matthew 6:19-20.

45

the mind as a computer terminal or radio receiver that can pick up thoughts from the universal consciousness.

We are not our emotions. Our emotions are the purview of our egos. Many emotions are the consequence of judging a thing or person to be good or bad, lovable or worthy of hate. Our emotions are closely related to our bodies. We can become addicted to the neuropeptides that are produced by our bodies in response to each emotion, which is explained well by the scientists in the movie *What the Bleep do We Know!?* [14]

Although each of these is a part of us, none of them is the full story of what we are. What, then, is left for us to identify with? That is the question we can answer only through our spiritual insights.

As conscious, sentient beings, we have the ability to observe our thoughts, our emotions, our bodies as independent entities and experiences. With practice we can learn to notice a thought arising or an emotion brewing. Exercising this ability helps lead to the spiritual insight of the pan-universal nature of our conscious awareness. As our consciousness rises, our primary identifications change.

Benefits

Faith in Unity, to any degree beyond our personal bodies and minds, is a powerful force for good in our world. It is

---

[14] Also see my comments in Chapter 3 about my addiction to shame.

fairly common to identify with our family and those closest to us. Some people also identify with their town, state, and country. Some will risk their own safety to go to war to defend their nation. Identification with the All is quite different, yet these other forms of wider identification are good stepping stones to that goal.

Universal Unity is the foundation of generosity and selflessness, and the foundation of the abundance paradigm, which states that "to give is to receive." When we are grounded in our spirit, unified with the All, we see that giving to others is really giving to ourselves, our larger Self. We are literally receiving as we give.

Unity is fully realized by only the most enlightened beings, yet this belief, which most of us can only conceptualize, is still helpful. Some of its benefits include:

- Realizing that giving is the same as receiving, which fosters graceful acceptance and generosity.
- Enabling a practice of radical acceptance, (see creed part 5) because the challenging behaviors of others are also a part of who we are.
- Realizing that God is always present as an aspect of ourselves.
- Support for environmental responsibility—we must protect all of nature as a practice of Self-preservation.

Because everything is fundamentally unified, each apparently separate manifestation is in constant flow of energy and information with every other manifestation. When we have the faith to accept this as our true reality, we begin to be comfortable "going with" and encouraging this "flow."

When understood and lived deeply, this first belief in fundamental Unity and Love supports and encompasses all my other beliefs.

Creed Part 2: Creation Theology and Devotion

If you often wonder about creation, this next part of my creed may be helpful to consider. Again, these are just suggested beliefs, not absolute truth that all readers should adopt. While my creed emphasizes belief in God, many people, some of them personal friends, do not believe in God and still live happy, productive lives, fully engaged with their communities and loved ones. They have found other beliefs to reinforce life practices. It is important for us to stay open to all ideas about God and creation, listening to our hearts and minds to see if they inspire us to modify our own faith-based beliefs. This openness, and possible modification, are important in all stages of our life's journey.

> **"The source of all manifestation is pure, energetic Pan-universal Consciousness.** God is the perfectly Loving co-creative relationship between diversified manifestations, and the relationship between all manifestations and Pan-universal Consciousness. i devote my life to God."

"Pan-universal Consciousness" refers to a concept in string theory (though he does not use this phrase), described by John Hagelin PhD[15] stating that universes are forming all the time out of pure, self-aware, consciousness. Popular mechanistic evolutionary theorists place original creation as happening once per universe, which for ours happened billions of years ago. They would say that after the Big Bang, mechanistic and atomic level forces took over to evolve the universe as we currently know it, including Earth and its life forms such as human beings. I believe, however, that (re)creation of the manifest from the un-manifest is an ongoing process consistent with the concept of wave / particle theory of matter as understood by quantum physics.

Many religions and cultures have creation stories that involve the beginning of humanity and how it came to be in this universe. These stories are usually at odds with modern scientific findings. While I don't think we need to know where we came from at a spiritual level in order to be happy and continue our spiritual journeys, the analytical part of my brain wants a plausible story. Therefore I have developed my own story, which borrows from and expands (spiritually) on John Hagelin's interpretation of string theory:

Before the Big Bang that created our universe, the Unity of the Pan-universal consciousness had not yet diversified, at least for our universe (there are believed

---

[15] He describes his theory in a YouTube video titled John Hagelin PhD on Consciousness (https://youtu.be/OrcWntw9juM accessed 8/28/17).

to be many). The Big Bang that created our universe, that started our round of physical manifestation, shattered some of that Pan-universal, Unified consciousness into semi-individualized spirits.

This story is consistent with my faith in Unity, and it inspired me to write this poem:

Universes Come and Go

Pan universal consciousness
with unified awareness
Entertaining the objective
Teaming with energy
a froth of space-time
is liken to the breath of a sleeping giant
automatic, effortless

Out of the froth springs a universe
born in an instant
Consciousness
very partially
quite temporarily
fragmenting

From the moment of birth
each manifest fragment
is drawn back to the One
Atoms joining into elements
as star dust raining down on cooler bodies
Throbbing with the energy of love lost
with a yearning to end separation from the Source
Elements joining into molecules

Molecules joining to give birth to life
Consciousness with a mind
a heart
a soul
facilitating the journey
Each mind receiving
the thoughts
of the One

Pin pricks of life
in a vast velvet fabric of space-time
through which consciousness perceives the manifest
After billions of orbits of billions of planets
enlightened fragments are still reuniting
Realizing they were never really separate
In the subjective adventure
of manifestation

In the end
entropy takes care of the rest
The cause of illusion is gone
Nothing can resist
the pull back to the Source
Unity is inevitable
continuous
reality

And the froth keeps burbling
fragments of consciousness
Universes manifesting like flakes of dandruff
itched off the head of a sleeping giant
floating on a breeze
some drawn right back into his mouth in the next
breath

some joining with nutrients in the ground
feeding plants in his garden
to be eaten later
but always rejoining
Nothing ever created
All is transforming
temporarily

Always returning from whence we came

"The source of all manifestation is pure, energetic Pan-universal Consciousness. **God is the perfectly Loving co-creative relationship between diversified manifestations, and the relationship between all manifestations and Pan-universal Consciousness.** i devote my life to God."

Because of fundamental Unity, God is everything and is the source of All. Every term is another name for (a part of) Pan-universal Unity. For thousands of years "God" has held powerful meanings for most people on earth. While I no longer find many of those meanings useful, I honor their power throughout the ages, so I like to include the term "God" in my faith.

By defining God as every relationship, I emphasize Unity and process, the relationships between Pan-universal consciousness, individualized consciousness and the manifest world, the relationships between manifestations, and the process of Loving creation, in which we play a part. The most powerful and fundamental relationship I know is Love, so Love is God and God is Love. In his email meditation of January 23, 2014, Friar Richard Rohr writes, "God is a mystery of relationship, and this relationship is foundationally and essentially love.[16]"

I believe God's Love is perfect, and that all creation has a perfect purpose to help diversified manifestations experience their source. Through Unity, we are each gods and goddesses incarnate. As "children" of God, the only difference between us and the greater all-inclusive unified God is our perception. We perceive ourselves to be separate, like children who have not yet taken on the responsibilities of adulthood. Unity with All is not a responsibility, it is our fundamental reality.

My concept of God is much like that of the Holy Spirit in Christianity. "God the Father" could be compared to Pan-universal consciousness and "The Son" likened to manifestation. It is a matter of semantics, which are only meaningful to the degree that they affect our actions or "works."

Jesus Christ said, "For where two or three are gathered in my name, there am I among them."[17] This is consistent with my definition of God as relationship. "In my name" refers to the conscious awareness of God's presence. That consciousness, which is more fundamental than we are, manifests through the co-creative relationship. When we are sharing physical space, we are creating our shared manifest reality in that space together.

[16] To sign up for Richard Rohr's daily email meditations go to https://cac.org

[17] Matthew 18:20

I was raised in the Episcopal church and required to go to confirmation class by my father, the son of an Episcopal Priest, the Reverend Hiram Kano. At the time I was agnostic, so was not confirmed. I'm sure grandpa Kano was disappointed. While my father said I did not have to believe everything verbatim, I disagreed. I could not stand in front of our whole congregation and recite the Apostles' Creed in good conscience. Now, ironically, my faith is in many ways similar and compatible with much of that creed.

Infinite Relationship

The Universe is like
One,
Unified
connect-the-dots puzzle:
    with page as consciousness,
    dots as manifestations,
    and lines,
    drawn by God.

Holistic lines
joining dots of all dimensions,
from sub-atomic
to astronomical.
All Creation
are Collectives,
held
by Divine Love.

Atoms
  of elements

         of molecules
          of cells
           of organisms
            of families
             of communities
              of ecosystems
               of worlds
                of solar systems
                 of galaxies
                  of universes
                   of Consciousness.

God binds All
in a co-creative embrace,
connecting the dots
to solve the puzzle
of consciousness,
manifesting.

Language allows us to articulate and contemplate the
relationship between things, our memories or the
memories of others and what we are experiencing today
and planning for in the future. Every word is defined by
other words in a vast linguistic web of relationship. Thus:

Nicknames

It has been said that Eskimos
have 50 words for snow,
and the Sami language
has 1,000 words for reindeer.
Although the former
may be a myth,

some things just have
more names.

Here's the grandest example,
of this linguistic
theme:
With hundreds of thousands
of words in each
of the thousands of languages,
there are
hundreds of millions
of words,
for God.

For me God is the whole enchilada, as they say, because
there can be no creation without relation. Behind and
before everything, our eternal relationship is to God.

> "The source of all manifestation is pure,
> energetic Pan-universal Consciousness. God is
> the perfectly Loving co-creative relationship
> between diversified manifestations, and the
> relationship between all manifestations and Pan-
> universal Consciousness. **i devote my life to
> God.**"

Devotion is a commitment to focus my attention. In *The
Seven Spiritual Laws of Success*, Deepak Chopra speaks of the
power of keeping your attention on your intention,
without becoming attached to the outcome.[18] Since God is

---

[18] Deepak Chopra, The Seven Spiritual Laws of Success: A
Practical Guide To the Fulfillment of Your Dreams (New
World Library, 1994), p. 70.

Love, we could also say that "i devote my life to Love." I intend to give my Love to the world, through actions that help any part of creation thrive. This last sentence uses the power of two words, devote and God, to state the spiritual intention by which I live. I like to use the word God instead of Love, because of the historical power attributed to the word, and because Love has so many different meanings.

God has many different meanings as well, which is why I include my definition before my intention of practice.

I have recently been a regular practicing member of "The Heart of the Valley" Mindfulness Practice Center in White River Junction. This center follows the teachings of Thich Nhat Hanh or "Thay," as we affectionately refer to him within that community. Of all the spiritual practices that Thay recommends, mindfulness is foremost. I have come to appreciate how mindfulness, as Thay describes it, is needed to be truly devout. Every moment lived in mindfulness is like a prayer of gratitude and holds infinite possibilities. In fact, mindfulness is needed for me to practice all the actions mentioned in my creed. I highly recommend his books and teachings.

Benefits

Faith in God as perfect Love is the foundation of love in every facet of my life. When I accept God's love as perfect, I see every moment of my life as a perfect creation, which brings me peace. Challenges, pain, and suffering present opportunities for growth. Even things my ego judges as "bad" are perfectly loving creations as well, co-created by God. Since I define God as a relationship between us and Pan-universal consciousness, we play a part in all creation. This faith, and a memory of my grandfather Kano saying that "everyone is perfect," inspired me to write this poem:

Total Surrender

Everyone is perfect
a guaranteed reflection
of their essence
just so

Our world is perfect
a collective creation
filling all needs
just so

The will of God
a karmic manifestation
continuous miracle
just so

We understand good
pray deliverance from evil
such is our fall
just so

Our good and evil
pleasure, pain and suffering
perfect creations
just so

> Surrender understanding
> release our judgments
> God's will is done
> just so

This poem does not mean that I think everything should stay the same as it is, that there is no room for improvement in the manifest world. It means that in the context of our current karmic stories God is co-creating exactly what we need. As our consciousness rises, the new perfect reflection will reveal the ego / judgmental view as even better than before that evolution of understanding. I'll be describing my beliefs in karma and consciousness later in this chapter.

We may think that the concept of Unity, and Love as God would preclude prayer. After all, to whom would we be praying? Prayer is a very powerful practice, so I've integrated it into my faith nonetheless. I pray to the love that is within each of us, that is our true essence. When I give thanks, I'm praying to the source of the law of karma (see part 5, below), which makes my life a perfect experience for this part of my journey. I am praying to the co-creative process in which we participate with every breath, through our relationship to Unity.

My standard "grace" before I eat, which I say to myself in silence as I hold hands with the others around the table, is "Dear God (of Love) thank you for this food. May it energize me in my perception of your perfect Love (or perfectly Loving presence)." God's Love is perfect, but it can be challenging to see that sometimes, so I pray for the ability to see it in all things and situations. As this book goes to press, this prayer has been answered, as described in the more recently written "About the Author" chapter.

The beauty of prayer is that it is personal for each of us. Everyone has his or her own appropriate prayers of thanks and hope. If I were going to pray for a better life, I'd pray for guidance in creating that life through actions that are in my best interests and the interests of those around me. There is no wrong way to pray, we need only use our imaginations.

The power of personal prayer is mindfulness. When we take the time to think of what to pray, for sources of gratitude, for example, we must be mindful in the process. I don't believe that we need to pray for God to "know" what we want or need. I have faith that God is beyond the need for our intellectual, individualized interpretations, even those of gratitude. God will automatically co-create what we need, regardless. Yet prayer feels really powerful, as an affirmation of my faith and a mindful ritual of gratitude. It helps remind me of my Unity with All.

Creed Part 3: Spiritual Beings, Reincarnation and Compassion

There are many ideas about life after death: heaven, hell, purgatory, reincarnation, or none of these—oblivion. While most living beings have some fear of death, those fears can contribute to making good choices or they can lead to irrational and less helpful beliefs. Deciding what we believe by staying open to all faith structures can help reduce unhelpful fears and contribute to a happy and peaceful life. This section of my creed provides examples of beliefs about life and death that I have found to be most useful.

> **"i am one of countless spiritual beings which manifest repeatedly as part of living Earth.** God willing, i will continue to reincarnate here until all earthly beings are free from suffering."

We are spiritual beings that existed before our current lives, and will continue to exist after we die. We live many lives through a process of reincarnation. In each life, we have opportunities to learn and progress at the spiritual level, in a journey that can take any number of lives to complete.

I have believed in reincarnation for many years, long enough to wonder about our spiritual relationship to life on other planets, which I believe must exist somewhere in our vast universe. In all the stories I've read about people who remember past lives, I've never heard of anyone recalling being an alien on another planet. Part of me wonders why this is the case. Once we are dead, what would stop us from reincarnating anywhere in the universe? I turned back to my primary faith in Unity for an answer.

We are fundamentally Unified and superficially diversified. I believe that the degree of our diversification does not include the ability to reincarnate on another planet. Each of us is a manifest **and** spiritual part of **this** planet. Stories that I have read, including many amazing ones from the work of Dr. Brian Weiss, Ian Stevenson and others, also indicate that we have soul mates that we tend to reincarnate with from one life to the next, and that we tend to reincarnate back into the same region of the world. This makes sense as another aspect of our Unity. I think of this as a continuum from individuality to Unity: a diversified spirit manifesting as an individual living (human) being is part of a group of two or more soul mates, which are members of a spiritual family, and are, subsequently, part of a spiritual community, part of all spiritual beings that make up a particular planet, part of all spiritual beings that make up a particular solar system, and part of all spiritual beings that make up a particular galaxy, that is, in turn, part of all the spiritual beings that manifest as a particular Universe. Finally, that Universe is part of all the manifest Universes that are each part of Pan-universal consciousness. The particular divisions in this example are arbitrary.

I was agnostic about reincarnation and life after death in general for many years, until I started to learn more about Tibetan Buddhism and its methods of finding the reincarnations of spiritual leaders or Rinpoches, including the Dalai Lama. As part of that method, they test candidate children to see if they recognize which of a large number of objects were owned by him in his previous life. Each object is presented along with a very similar one that was not owned by the him. If the candidate can pick the correct objects they are that much closer to being accepted as the current incarnation. The fact that this process has been used for many generations seems to me to be strong evidence of reincarnation. Then I read some of Dr. Brian Weiss's books.

Weiss is a traditional psychotherapist who did not believe in reincarnation until he experienced many of his patients recalling past life traumas during hypnotic regressions. His stories sealed my faith in reincarnation, which has been further strengthened by its significant benefits to my life, outlined below.

Some find the work of Dr. Ian Stevenson even more compelling, because he interviewed thousands of children who claimed to have memories of their past lives, without the aid of hypnosis. The book *Old Souls*, by journalist Tom Shroder, helped to reinforce my belief in reincarnation. The book takes the reader along with Shroder as he traveled with Dr. Stevenson on one of his research trips.

> "i am one of countless spiritual beings which manifest repeatedly as part of living Earth. **God willing, i will continue to reincarnate here**

until all earthly beings are free from suffering."

Buddhists believe that when a person reaches Enlightenment, his or her spirit is free to end its cycle of reincarnation. Spirits may reincarnate again, but they have some choice in the matter. I have not studied this belief in depth, but I like it enough to incorporate it into my faith. If I do have a choice, I'd prefer to continue to have additional lives, regardless of my realizing Enlightenment in this lifetime. This preference affirms my love of life and my devotion to my planet, of which I'm an integral part.

Since I believe in Unity, when any part of planet Earth suffers, I naturally want to help by reducing the pain and/or shedding light on the optional nature of attachment, without which we can experience pain without suffering. This is the insight of compassion.

As I prepared to move into Koinonia Farm for a one-year internship, I wondered how my belief in reincarnation would affect my ability to integrate and share my (related) beliefs in a Christian setting, where people believe in one life followed by eternity in heaven (or hell). I began to think, "How can billions of people with faith in one life followed by heaven all be wrong? Could these seemingly incompatible beliefs both be right, at least to some degree?" Three weeks into my internship, this question gelled into an insight worth sharing.

How can a person "go to heaven" but still be reincarnated? The answer is simple: their spiritual essence can be in "two places" at once. Christians talk of the spirit of God within and how God holds all of his children in a loving embrace. This is the insight of spiritual unity with God that is shared by mystics and monastics from all major religious traditions. Perhaps this understanding is best thought of as including unity between heaven and earthly creation, even for each semi-individualized soul. Each of us could be "in heaven" while simultaneously experiencing creation through the senses of our current bodies here on earth. Perhaps we are all residing in heaven (or hell) for eternity and only superficially and temporarily manifesting as separate physical beings.

Jesus taught Christians to pray, "Our Father, who art in heaven, hallowed be Thy name. Thy kingdom come, Thy will be done, on earth as it is in heaven...." which is the start of what we now call "The Lord's Prayer." I used to interpret this as being a prayer of hope for the heavenly peace of God to become manifest on earth. Now, I prefer to believe that Jesus was really saying God's will is always being done in every moment, "on earth as it is in heaven." In other words, what is happening in each moment of creation is a reflection of our spiritual nature in heaven (and hell). He could have been saying that the kingdom of God has already come and is coming to earth in every moment. If there is an aspect of supplication in this prayer, it is meant to ask that the spiritual nature of our collective being may become more enlightened. That Enlightenment may help some to avoid "living hells" and help them live more through Christ's teachings and those of other enlightened prophets from different faith traditions. In Buddhist terms, this can be seen as seeking Enlightenment while serving others until all earthly suffering has ceased.

Benefits

Reincarnation can be seen as a foundation of fearlessness. In his book *Love Is Letting Go Of Fear*, Gerald G. Jampolski outlines the concept that every emotion, every thought, everything we do, comes from fear or love. These, he believes, are the only true emotions and motivations. When we let go of fear, we naturally open ourselves to love. I believe that the fear of death is the root of all fears, thus letting this go is essential to freeing ourselves from other fears.

For example, we understandably fear rejection. In past generations, total rejection from the group upon which you depended was tantamount to a death sentence. We are social animals, so loneliness evokes fear of vulnerability. A faith foundation of Unity and immortality helps me realize that I am never alone, can never really die, and therefore can experience every moment as it comes. Openness to adopt beliefs from more than just a single religion is key to freeing myself from these fears.

For example, Christians believe in love as the primary teaching of Jesus, and they also believe in one life, followed by either heaven or hell. This belief structure tends to lead people to live their lives in fear—fear of death and fear of the unknown. Will we go to heaven, or have our sins been unforgivable? Even if Christians are sure they will get into heaven, what will that be like? The unknown is always scarier than the known. Even those with a strong faith in the promise of heaven still fear death because it is the end of all they know. And if one only gets one life, then it is natural to want it to be as long as possible. Therefore, belief in reincarnation offers the comfort of knowing that when we die it is just a new beginning—death followed by rebirth—another chance to live again.

The other tendency of the belief in a single life followed by heaven is the feeling, and even lifestyle, of preparation, planning and anticipation of the rewards to come in paradise. This is only a tendency for some and certainly not the intention of the teachings of Christianity or Judaism. But I believe it is an inherent weakness of these beliefs. I think living for the future, or acting out of fear or anticipation of rewards, is not the true way of Love.

With the belief in reincarnation, rebirth may actually be scarier than death. There is evidence that people remember their past lives after death. Some people who have died and been brought back to life recount their experiences in great detail. They knew who they were and remember the welcoming white light. But most of us don't remember our past lives, so we assume that babies don't either. With this understanding, it is at birth that we would loose the memories of our previous life, not when we die. With faith strong enough to identify with our spiritual Selves, we can see that our fundamental selves are much more than our experiences and memories of the physical world.

Reincarnation is also the foundation of acceptance and compassion. When we believe that we have all experienced past lives, some filled with hatred, violence and spiritual ignorance, we can identify with and have compassion for others who struggle with these feelings and experiences. When we meet a more loving and peaceful person, we can see ourselves in them, with faith that one day we too will reach their level of understanding and grace. When we believe we are all experiencing one part of a common journey, we are more willing to learn from spiritual leaders and serve as good examples to others. We can see and feel in our hearts how we are truly in this together, which brings us back to Love.

Much of the peace derived from faith in reincarnation depends on an appreciating one's life enough to want to have another. Perhaps the Christian belief of a single life is more comforting for people who have more suffering than joy in their lives. Therefore, Christian faith foundations (at least about life after death) might be more appropriate for you, but that might not always be the case. My creed asks for flexibility and the willingness to rebuild our foundations when they no longer serve us as well as they have in the past.

We live in an era of global crisis and multiple challenges: human overpopulation, a debt-based monetary system with unsustainable growth imperative, climate change, deforestation, species extinction, and more. We need to work together to slow or reverse these trends or we are likely to face changes that come at us faster than we can cope with them, causing devastation and suffering across the planet. Some of these challenges are already occurring to some degree, such as drought, floods, mass crop failures, economic collapse, famine, and more. Without my faith, it would be difficult for me to avoid despair.

A faith foundation that emphasizes identification with our beautiful planet helps me to live more responsibly. I'm here for the long haul, life after life into the foreseeable future. The actions I take that affect our planet will also affect my semi-individualized self in subsequent lives.

Creed Part 4: Raising Consciousness and Meditation

The fourth part of my creed supports my most important and long-standing practice: twice daily silent sitting meditation. There are many scientifically proven benefits of meditating every day: stress relief, improved mental abilities, improved quality of sleep and relief from insomnia, and many more. For years I meditated twice a day to relieve stress. This chapter explains how my current faith supports this practice because of its longer term benefits.

> **"Fundamental qualities in the life of a diversified spiritual being, such as happiness, compassion, grace, insight, and love, reflect each being's level of consciousness.** It is the nature of manifest consciousness to rise in time from shame to Enlightenment. Mindfulness meditation facilitates this process. i will practice silent sitting meditation at least twice a day."

Illusions masquerading as reality often cloud our ability to see the beautiful context of our lives. As we clear away these illusions, our consciousness rises and our lives improve. The most complete descriptions of this process I know are by David R. Hawkins, MD, PhD, author of many books on the spiritual journey, including *Power vs. Force*. He has identified God view, Life view, Emotion and Process for each of 17 levels of consciousness on a logarithmic scale from 1 to 1000. The scale shows how the quality of a person's life increases with consciousness. I prefer to think of a person's level of consciousness as a range of levels and a tendency to live closer to one level than others. For example, a person at a moderately high level of consciousness may still feel ashamed from time to time, but that is different from living a life crippled by low self-esteem.

> "Fundamental qualities in the life of a diversified spiritual being, such as happiness, compassion, grace, insight, and love, reflect each being's level of consciousness. **It is the nature of manifest consciousness to rise in time from shame to Enlightenment.** Mindfulness meditation facilitates this process. i will practice silent sitting meditation at least twice a day."

Life is about the journey back to our source, back to Divine Love, to realization of Pan-universal Unity. Buddhists call it "Enlightenment," or that state that enables a person to realize their true being as unity with All.

This spiritual journey starts at a lower level of consciousness and proceeds to higher levels. We all ultimately reach spiritual Enlightenment after innumerable lifetimes and are then freed from the cycle of reincarnation. We sometimes regress before we can advance again, but the process is fundamental and ongoing. This is the ancient Buddhist belief, in a nutshell.

Unity In Time

If you believe Enlightenment
is better than shame
(even though you won't admit it to your friends).

Then you must believe tomorrow
is better than yesterday,
and a grandparent is better
than a newborn babe.

No wait, you think,
what could be more precious?
Who could compare
to sweet innocence?

You've heard the sages' lesson
that everything is part
of the Unity you seek.
Each Moment
is Unified
as well.
All ends and their beginnings
are equally Blessed.

In Truth
you're feeling shame,
and you are Enlightened,

Now,
only now.

This poem emphasizes and illustrates how our fundamental Unity means that we are actually Enlightened already, we just have not realized it yet. Even though it is true, it may not be real to us. The ego is in the way, wanting only to experience lower consciousness aspects of our larger selves. When we see time, which advanced physics tells us was created along with matter by the Big Bang, as an illusion, we can eventually see ourselves as Unified with every moment in time and with every level of consciousness we have and will experience.

Timelessness

Time creates half
of the grand illusion,
that enables the dance of life.
Manifestation diversifies consciousness,
time diversifies soul.

In the age-old journey
from confusion to Unity,
your soul is much transformed.
Memories of yesterday
and dreams of tomorrow,
cloud reality,
today.
Vast possibilities in quality of being,
take time for you to realize.

Yet your soul is Unified
with each step in time
and All the manifest world.
You can only be
what You
are Now.
This may be why it has been said,
you are already Enlightened!

As human beings we have wonderful opportunities for spiritual growth. But this growth is challenged by our ego. Our ego says that our survival in this life is paramount. That little reptilian part of our brain we inherited from our early evolutionary ancestors says that the world is a dangerous place, where we will perish if we're not always on guard. While awareness of physical threats is important for making good decisions—such as keeping our eyes on the road when we drive—awareness can sometimes become fear, extending into our spiritual lives and standing in the way of love.

When we maintain mindful awareness of our spiritual Selves, we can become more fearless, graceful and loving.

"Fundamental qualities in the life of a diversified spiritual being, such as happiness, compassion, grace, insight, and love, reflect each being's level of consciousness. It is the nature of manifest consciousness to rise in time from shame to Enlightenment. **Mindfulness meditation facilitates this process.** i will practice silent sitting meditation at least twice a day."

Meditation has been shown to be helpful in relieving stress and facilitating subtle awareness of thoughts as they arise. Reduced stress helps us respond to our situation more gracefully. When we become familiar with how our thoughts arise, it is easier to mindfully notice a thought before we react in response. Many of our thoughts are not helpful, especially when acting on them causes suffering. Dr. David Hawkins goes so far as to say, "All thinking, from a spiritual viewpoint, is merely vanity, illusion, and pomposity. The less one thinks, the more delightful life becomes."[19] For decades I found that meditation did not help me reduce the number of thoughts I had in any given period of time, though it does help support my other spiritual practices of loving kindness and mindfulness. Through mindful "I am" practice over the last two plus years, the number of thoughts I tend to have has greatly reduced and they seem "quieter" than before. I can now affirm Dr. Hawkins's statement that having fewer thoughts does indeed make life more delightful!

Buddhist masters have often taught that we don't meditate to "become Enlightened," we do it for its own sake, and they have reinforced that statement by saying we already are Enlightened, as articulated in my poem earlier in this chapter, "Timelessness." I suspect they say this because attachment is the main cause of suffering, which can often stand in the way of spiritual progress. Attachment in this context means identifying with something so strongly that it is imagined to be a necessary part of who you are. It is one of many spiritual paradoxes:

---

[19] David Hawkins, Discovery of the Presence of God (Veritas Publishing 2006), p. 89, Kindle Edition loc. 1200.

we can never reach a spiritual goal to which we are attached, so we must find other motivations for our discipline.

> "Fundamental qualities in the life of a diversified spiritual being, such as happiness, compassion, grace, insight, and love, reflect each being's level of consciousness. It is the nature of manifest consciousness to rise in time from shame to Enlightenment. Mindfulness meditation facilitates this process. **i will practice silent sitting meditation at least twice a day.**"

Consistent practice is important. Some people say that to maintain one's level of consciousness, meditating once a day is enough, but to make progress requires two. I don't know whether I agree. Any amount of meditation is better than none. Those who are new to daily meditation can even try just five or ten minutes a day to start, for example, when they first wake up in the morning, or just before they go to sleep at night.

Personal Story: Starting to Meditate

My freshman year in high school was rough. The end of 8th grade saw me rebelling against my former self, who always did his homework as soon as he got home: I stopped doing it altogether. As I came into puberty, I realized my network of friends was very thin, and I was not happy. My transition into high school marked my focus on making and keeping friends.

I don't remember just how it happened, but I ended up friends with folks that loved to party. We loved our beer.

We smoked a lot of pot. Sometimes we even got high during school. My grades suffered. My life became stressful, at least when I was not high. I believe the stress was what led to my first significant symptoms of the bipolar illness that I would admit, decades later, was part of my life.

I got rather depressed, in a kind of paranoid way. In the spring I was given the lead role in the musical *Peter Pan*, and I thought the stage crew was out to get me. They were constructing a system of wires and pulleys that would allow us to fly, and accidents were happening, although it was the stage crew and technical director that were getting hurt, not the actors. But I was worried and started to behave very strangely.

By the end of my first year in high school, I was a mess. I made it through *Peter Pan* well enough, but it would be my last lead role: the director would never again want to risk a repeat performance of my unreliable behavior. I was failing or barely passing my classes, but I did not care. I was angry, or I was stoned. My parents insisted that I get some counseling and I reluctantly agreed. It did not help much, but going forced me to admit that I had a problem. Something had to be done.

One spring weekend when I was visiting our summer home in Cape Cod, my friends in the York family invited me to go with them to an upcoming introductory lecture on Transcendental Meditation. Since they were good friends, I trusted it was worth checking out. The introduction was on a weeknight a couple of weeks later, so I had to take the bus back to Cape Cod to attend. By the end of that session, we were all motivated to sign up for the rest of the course. So on June 10, 1972, my friend Andrea and I got our initiation and started to meditate twice a day. I've been doing one form or another of silent sitting meditation twice a day ever since.

This was the first of many turning points in my life that were at least partly motivated by my mental illness. It was a wonderful example of how a difficult situation could lead to a positive, life-changing new beginning.

Benefits

Every qualitative aspect of life depends on our level of consciousness, so the benefits of this belief and the practices that they support are too many to list. I believe that raising consciousness is the fundamental way of gaining any wholesome, worthwhile benefit.

Bully in a Bar Room

My ego was like a bully,
in a dark bar room.

Back when I thought
that it was me,
I feared the losses,
defended my views,
took the dares,
broke my bones,
and loved the thrills.

Yes,
those were the rowdy days!

Eventually I could distinguish,
my Self,
from it,
but we were still like twins,
joined at the hip.
Even though I knew it,
I could not control it,
nor could I get away.
Every time I went out for a drink,
there it was again,
making a stink.

When we went on the wagon,
I loosened its grip.
By stepping away,
I discerned some space,
while still in that bar,
with its ruckus and mace.

After years of getting
juice at that bar,
that felt so much like home,
I finally stepped back out the door,
and let the bully go.
Its noisy thoughts grew quieter,
and easier to counter,
before it took hold of me
and steered my life asunder.

I still visit
that bar sometimes,
and even take part
in its fights,
but more and more often

I just shrug off
that noisy voice inside.

Yes, I still have an ego,
or else I would be dead.
But now it's more like
a two year old:
clever and willful
but harmless,
and good at reminding
me,
how very unhappy
folks can be,
when they take their egos
too seriously.

After over four decades of meditation, I have found some level of mastery over my ego. Most adults have learned some self-control, which is similar to what I'm describing in this poem: we don't grab an object out of another person's hand and rip it away as soon as we desire it for our own use. We learned some patience and manners as we socialized with our peers, hopefully with plenty of help from our parents and other caretakers. As we raise our consciousness, we have more control over our minds as well as our actions. We can "turn down the volume" on thoughts that we see as disturbing our peace of mind, on thoughts that could lead to more suffering if they were followed into actions. The lower our consciousness, the more likely we are to act on a thought immediately, before the possible consequences have been weighed. On later reflection we often regret these "knee jerk" reactions.

In many of our mainstream cultures, pride is considered a virtue. It certainly is, as compared to shame, anger or hopelessness, but compared to Love or even reason, it could be considered an error. On Hawkins's scale of consciousness, pride is just below the critical level of "Truth and Falsehood" (which on his scale of 1-1000 is at 200), with courage the next level above. As my appreciation of this grew, it inspired this poem:

Before The Fall

Pride in past achievements
Can keep us on track
When following our passions
A pat on the back

Seductive is this feeling
That keeps us on the go
It helps support identity
Until we finally know

God's love is unconditional
Our hearts feel this is true
Unlike this self-judgment
Comparing me to you

So celebrate successes
We manifest each day
Release the separate credit
As we walk the humble way

Creed Part 5: Karma and Forgiveness

I like "knowing" how things work. I was raised by a mechanical engineer who could explain how just about any physical thing worked—and often did, when asked. So as my questions expanded to the realms of the universal, I wanted my creed to include at least some explanations of the mysterious mechanisms God uses to co-create our world. Like the rest of my creed, this is offered as a suggestion only. I highly recommend the practice of forgiveness, but like any other helpful practices it can be supported by many beliefs and motivations.

> **"i am superficially human.** my actions co-create my world and sow the karmic seeds of what i will eventually reap. Each moment is a perfect response to our karma, which contains many opportunities to learn and grow in Love. When i fail to love, i will cherish the opportunity to forgive and affirm my devotion to God."

I am superficially a human being, at least for this life, because fundamentally I'm unified with All. I like including this in my creed to remind myself not to be too attached to my current life nor my current species, which are temporary manifestations in a larger context of spiritual reality. Yet even the superficial aspect of what I am has a beautiful role to play.

> "i am superficially human. **my actions co-create my world and sow the karmic seeds of what i will eventually reap.** Each moment is a perfect response to our karma, which contains many opportunities to learn and grow in Love. When i fail to love, i will cherish the opportunity to forgive and affirm my devotion to God."

God's Love is perfect. Everything that manifests is on its journey back to Unity, and is a perfect reflection of a part of God. My concept of karma is consistent with my belief that everything in this moment is exactly as it should be, to help fulfill the needs in our spiritual journeys. Christians say "God moves in mysterious ways" because when we feel pain, we often point to events around us that seem unloving, or even cruel and/or unjust. Our karma stems not only from our current lives but from our past ones as well. So, when we feel pain, we can gain insight into an aspect of our past that we usually don't remember, because we always reap what we sow.

This is the second time I've used the word "co-creat(ive)" in my creed. The first was "God is the perfectly Loving co-creative relationship..." in the second part of my creed. (See "Creed Part 2: Creation Theology and Devotion"). My level of consciousness and karma set the stage for God to help me create, (or me to help God create) exactly what I need in each moment of my life. The manifest reality springs from Pan-universal consciousness in each moment through this co-creative process, orchestrated by God.

In my current life, I've suffered from shame, especially over my inability to easily memorize and recall some things. I was judged as lacking by my father when I was in 3rd grade, as he attempted to help me memorize my multiplication tables. For three nights in a row he drilled me, and each night was more fearful for me than the one before. Since then, up until about the age of 50, I feared forgetting people's names and faces in particular, and everything else in general. That fear, both of forgetting and of being judged as less than for my poor memory, has at times been paralyzing. So I believe that in my previous life times, I also judged others as lesser or lacking, causing them shame. My karma matched my parents' tendencies, who each provided me with lessons I needed to learn in this life. Just like lessons regarding the physical world (don't touch the wood stove), spiritual lessons are often painful. So my faith has allowed me to forgive them. I am grateful for every opportunity I have to move closer to reuniting with my source, even when painful.

> "i am superficially human. my actions co-create my world and sow the karmic seeds of what i will eventually reap. **Each moment is a perfect response to our karma, which contains many opportunities to learn and grow in Love.** When i fail to love, i will cherish the opportunity to forgive and affirm my devotion to God."

I want to take responsibility for my current situation, which I have co-created for myself and those around me. One day in a time of family crisis someone yelled at me, saying, "You created this, David!" I affirmed, "Yes, I did!" What I did not add, was that I was not acting alone. Each and every one of us, all of creation, plays a part in co-creating our realities with God. God insures that we are given the karmic lessons we need based on our past actions and our current level of consciousness. Each of us is reaping what we have sown and, to some extent, what those around us have sown as well. Co-creation is a unified process that includes too many factors for us to comprehend. It is best not to even try, so I put my faith in God as I strive to love every moment and all of creation.

Personal Story: Karma & Honesty

The man stood over me in a small, plain room. He said, "This machine is not a lie detector, it's a polygraph. If there is a lie detector in this room, it's me. I can tell if you are lying." I assured him I had no intention of lying, as I was innocent.

Several years before, when I was a sophomore in high school, I received a refund check in the mail. I had placed a $10 deposit on a number of stereo components at a store in Cambridge, Massachusetts, which I hoped my parents would buy for my birthday. The man at the store promised me the sale price if I left a deposit, and a refund if my parents decided the equipment was not their first choice for my gift. To my disappointment, I called the store a few days later asking for my deposit back.

When the check arrived I was surprised to see the amount was over $200. Evidently, they had made a clerical error and sent me the purchase price of the components instead of my small deposit. I was not sure what to do:

keep the money or notify them of their mistake. I asked my parents that evening. The three of us were in the kitchen when I told them what happened and of my quandary over what to do. My dad said, "You could wait for a while to see if they notice the mistake before you cash it!" to which my mom replied, "No you can't, you have to send it back!" My father immediately reversed his position saying that of course my mother was right. Honesty was the best and only policy.

I placed the check, in its envelope, back into the place in my kitchen cubby where I had kept it, feeling stupid to have asked my parents in the first place. I wanted to keep the money, but I was nervous about the prospect. Now that they had said it was wrong, I thought I would be in double jeopardy if I did. I left the check in my cubby for several days and conferred with each of my friends.

All of them thought I would be crazy to return the check. That money represented lots of party time and fun for us. They just questioned the best strategy for moving forward. In the end I did cash it, by opening a new passbook savings account. The bank was in Sudbury, Massachusetts, close to town where we often went to the local sub shop or Friendly's restaurant to eat. Since I lived in the neighboring town of Lincoln, there was little chance my mother would ever see me doing business at the bank, and the account did not send statements, as the balance was always visible in the passbook.

For quite a few months I chipped away at my ill-gotten funds, mostly to purchase pot for me and my friends. It was nice to be the generous source of our party fun. The store never caught their error, or if they did, they wrote off the money without so much as contacting me.

Several years later, I was traveling in Florida for the winter to practice windsurfing. I was running low on funds so I got a job washing dishes at a small restaurant near the beach in Venice. The owner was a nice young man in a new marriage. His wife worked behind the counter. There were two employees: the chef and me. I worked hard at my assignments, which often led to praise at the thorough job I did on the tough items. Until the hammer fell.

One day my boss followed me out to my car, asking to talk privately. He said that he understood how hard it must be living in my car on a shoestring and washing dishes for a living. He could see how if I was faced with temptation, I might do something I would regret. I had no idea what he was leading up to, when he said that several hundred dollars had been stolen from him that week. Evidently, his wife had left a money bag in the kitchen one night and it was gone when she returned the next morning. The chef was a long-time trusted employee and I was the new kid. I was the windsurfing bum, so it made the most sense to him that I had taken the money.

I was crushed. I thought the man had become my friend and I couldn't believe he would accuse me of stealing. I had not even been aware of the opportunity. In a fit of confusion and fear, I started to cry. He took this as a sign of guilt, and asked me where I put the money. Between sobs, I repeated that I did not take the money, that he could search my car if he wanted. But he was unsatisfied, saying that I could have hidden it anywhere by now. I felt very vulnerable so far from home with few resources or friends to turn to for help.

Since I was so adamant of my innocence, my boss agreed to pay for a lie detector test. If I passed he would believe me and I could keep my job while they looked further for the thief. If I failed they would press charges and I'd be fired.

The polygraph operator, aka "human lie detector" asked the usual benign questions to get data and a feel for how I reacted to questions to which I answered truthfully: my name, hometown, etc. As he led up to the crucial question, I found myself remembering that refund check back in my high school days. I felt nervous and a bit guilty, because I remembered depositing the refund check sent to me in error.

I failed the test. I explained to my boss how I was feeling guilty about an old transgression and he even let me take it over again. I failed again. After all those years, I was paying for my dishonesty. My karma had caught up with me, after all.

Since I was innocent, they never could prove otherwise and I just lost my job, but ever since that experience I've been quite strict with myself about honesty. I also had a new personal experience with the concept of karma, strengthening my faith in this belief.

> "i am superficially human. my actions co-create my world and sow the karmic seeds of what i will eventually reap. Each moment is a perfect response to our karma, which contains many

opportunities to learn and grow in Love. **When i fail to love, i will cherish the opportunity to forgive and affirm my devotion to God.**"

As a fallible human being, I will sometimes judge others as wrong or bad, as my ability to love them falters. This is always caused by a misunderstanding and/or lack of compassion for their situation. Judgment without forgiveness, of myself or of others, causes suffering. So this intention of a practice of forgiveness is very important. Life is challenging enough without carrying long-term judgments against myself or others.

Over the course of a couple of decades, I wrote a trilogy of poems related to forgiveness. The first one, from 1986, is:

Practice

Love grows
　　Stronger when you share it
Forgiveness
　　The key to love's success
Practice
　　Makes forgiving easy
Time
　　Is free for all to spend

If we have trouble forgiving, practice can help. The second poem, from 2011, is:

Acceptance

Forgiveness
    is a gift
Presented
    to both parties
Acceptance
    is required to grow
Love
    frees us from judgment

This illustrates that forgiveness is not only for the person being forgiven. It actually benefits the person doing the forgiving even more. The 3rd poem, also written in 2011, is:

Judgment's End

Let judgment cease
Forgiveness, obsolete
Energy for love expands
Bliss!

The more judgmental we are, the more difficult it is for us to practice forgiveness. If we can intellectually believe in karmic mechanisms and a loving God, we can have faith that difficult situations are as they should be, even as our emotions are raging. The belief can help to cool our anger and start the sometimes long process of forgiveness, because forgiveness is always possible, but will not happen unless we make some effort. Even a transgression we have "forgotten" can carry with it emotional memories that will hinder our happiness, unless we have found forgiveness.

Benefits

The belief in karma and a perfectly loving God are foundations of grace. When we have faith that this moment is exactly as it should be, it is easy to accept even painful situations. I may not understand how I have come to the events in my life, but faith can give me the patience to stay open for those answers over time, in loving acceptance and grace. In fact, the stronger my faith, the fewer answers I require. In the end of our spiritual journeys, all questions fall away when a deeper truth is revealed.

This grace can extend to our experiences and relationships to others as well. Without a belief in possible greater purposes for pain and suffering, it is easy to become overwhelmed when fully experiencing our world. I remember a time when my despair over a perceived injustice tore a hole in an otherwise beautiful, peaceful day.

Personal Story: Karma and Peace of Mind

Years ago, I was on a weekend-long sailing cruise with my then-girlfriend Joy on her friend's 33-foot sloop off the coast of Maine. We had stopped for the night in a lovely inner harbor and had gone ashore to explore the small town and purchase some take-out lobster for dinner on the boat. It had been a beautiful summer day and the sun was starting to feel cooler in the early evening hours. After we got the food I took a longer route through the town to further enjoy the peaceful neighborhoods, as Joy and her friend went straight back to the boat ahead of me.

As I walked down a narrow residential road lined with cottages, I heard a child crying and approached a scene with a clearly angry woman shouting at a toddler. I had not been witness to what had caused the upset, but the woman had evidently been trying to get the boy to do something without success. He was rooted to the grass, crying hard as she made her anger and frustration known by her words and the tenseness of her body language. She may have been trying to get him to go inside, because before I'd made it past their yard she declared that she and the rest of the children were going inside without him. She ordered the rest of them in and left him crying by himself by the side of the road.

At this point I stopped walking, having just passed their house, distressed that anyone would abandon their child. Then I saw her peeking out of the edge of the door occasionally, taking care that the child would not see her. I desperately wanted to do something to comfort the child, but I knew that as a stranger I had few options that would be acceptable to the woman. I resolved to stay within view of the child, so he could see me and I could keep an eye on him as well, so he would not feel quite so alone. I did my best to send him my compassion and love from a distance and waited for the situation to resolve. Eventually, she came back out and brought the boy back inside with her.

As I continued to walk back to the boat, I was fuming with anger at the woman for the possibly life-long harm she had just done to that child. Abandonment is one of our innate fears. When we are abandoned as children, the fear can extend into our adult lives in ways that continue to challenge us until we find healing ways to recover. I wondered if her actions, if repeated habitually, would be deemed grounds for Family Services to step in to protect the child from abuse. My heart felt the need to find solutions to the situation, because the injustice seemed so uncalled for and damaging. But I knew as a stranger visiting the community, I was powerless to get involved. When I recounted the experience to Joy and her friend and we discussed the issues that it raised, I finally broke down and wept. We knew that this child's experience was certainly not unique and having just experienced this horror, I could not bear the thought of it being commonplace.

With my current faith in a perfectly loving God and the karmic law which provides the experiences we need to learn from our past actions, I no longer feel the need to step in and "fix" every injustice I witness. My heart still goes out to the child in the shopping cart when his or her mother is stressed out enough to be angrily snapping judgmental phrases. My heart goes out to the mother, too, and when I feel there is nothing I can do to help, I can find peace again by reminding myself that their stressful moments are as perfect for them as my peaceful moments are for me. Their lives are taking them through their own lessons, hard as they may be.

With this belief it is perhaps all the more important to recognize when there are some actions I can take that could help reduce the suffering of others. The last thing I want to do is use my faith in God and karma as an excuse for inaction in the face of injustice. Every situation met with suffering is also an opportunity for witnesses to take compassionate actions, even if they are simply prayers of support from a distance.

In an interview with Oprah Winfrey, Thich Nhat Hanh was asked how he can reconcile peace of mind with knowledge of all the suffering in the world. He used the metaphor of a beautiful lotus flower growing out of the mud. He said both suffering and happiness "inter-are." "So suffering is the kind of mud that we must be able to use in order to grow the flower of compassion and happiness."[20]

[20] Interview on YouTube: http://youtu.be/NJ9UtuWfs3U (accessed 9/4/2017).

Creed Part 6: Discernment and Radical Acceptance

Implementation of my intentions to serve require a decision-making process I can trust. Everyone uses some kind of process to make decisions, large and small, every day—many of them unconscious, some conscious. Each of us may be happy with the process we use, or we may want to try something new. It's always up to us: they are our belief systems and decisions. There is no one right way to do anything, but there is at least one way that will work for each of us. Heart-based decisions, in the context of radical acceptance, just happen to work for me. Let's see why.

> "my heart can feel the Loving mind of God. The process of discernment, through radical acceptance of everyone I meet and of all creation, helps to reveal actions which reduce suffering. i will follow my heart in a practice of grateful acceptance."

Many spiritual teachers agree, and now modern science has determined that the heart contains more neuron cells than muscle cells! The heart is both a thinking and a blood pumping organ. This is important, because our minds are easily fooled. In *Discovery of the Presence of God*, David Hawkins says, "The fundamental innocence of mankind is based on the reality that the human mind is incapable of discerning truth from falsehood.[21]" So the best decision-making process utilizes feelings from the heart.

In *The Seven Spiritual Laws of Success* Deepak Chopra writes:

> Consciously put your attention in the heart and ask your heart what to do. Then wait for the response—a physical response in the form of a sensation. It may be the faintest level of feeling—but it's there, in your body. Only the heart knows the correct answer. Most people think the heart is mushy and sentimental. But it's not. The heart is intuitive, it's holistic, it's contextual, it's relational. ... At times it may not even seem rational, but the heart has a computing ability that is far more accurate and far more precise than anything within the limits of rational thought.[22]

"my heart can feel the Loving mind of God. **The process of discernment, through radical acceptance of everyone I meet and of all**

---

[21] David R. Hawkins, Discovery of the Presence of God (Veritas Publishing, 2006), p. 27, Kindle Edition loc. 271.

[22] Deepak Chopra, The Seven Spiritual Laws of Success: A Practical Guide To the Fulfillment of Your Dreams (New World Library, 1994), p. 43-44.

creation, helps to reveal actions which reduce suffering. i will follow my heart in a practice of grateful acceptance."

Acceptance is a powerful spiritual practice that is required to fully develop my ability to be compassionate and Love unconditionally. Jesus taught this lesson, which starts, "Judge not, that you not be judged."[23] This lesson affirms our Unity, as do many of his teachings when read with faith in this ultimate reality. Because of that Unity, judging another is quite literally judging an aspect of your true, largest Self. Also note the unqualified nature of this teaching, which itself is quite "radical."

Again, Deepak Chopra writes,

> Another way to access the field of pure potentiality is through the practice of non-judgment. Judgment is the constant evaluation of things as right or wrong, good or bad. When you are constantly evaluating, classifying, labeling, analyzing, you create a lot of turbulence in your internal dialogue. This turbulence constricts the flow of energy between you and the field of pure potentiality.[24]

Chopra uses the term "field of pure potentiality" to describe what I'm calling "pan-universal consciousness."

---

[23] Matthew 7:1-5.

[24] Deepak Chopra, The Seven Spiritual Laws of Success: A Practical Guide To the Fulfillment of Your Dreams (New World Library, 1994), p. 17.

When I learned this practice from Chopra, I too called it non-judgment. In the years since 1996 when I started this practice, I've come to realize the problematic nature of the term. This practice can be one of the most difficult ones to "master," so if we don't have patience we can find ourselves in judgment of ourselves for our continued judgmental tendencies! This is clearly not helpful to the process. When we fail to accept everything that is happening in this moment, we can simply accept our abilities to do the practice as they are while we work towards radical acceptance of everything, regardless of how much pain and suffering are involved.

> "my heart can feel the Loving mind of God. The process of discernment, through radical acceptance of everyone I meet and of all creation, helps to reveal actions which reduce suffering. **i will follow my heart in a practice of grateful acceptance.**"

Judgments against others and ourselves are always based on misunderstandings, ignorance and/or fear. If we deeply understand another person, we cannot judge them harshly. If we truly understand ourselves, we will feel self-love instead of shame, even when we make mistakes that seem to be the cause of our or another's pain. Negative judgments stand in the way of unconditional Love, which is our true nature given to us by God.

This section of my creed and its intention of practice reinforces the previous more fundamental ones. Yet it is important because the ego tends to be very judgmental. It leans towards decisions that create challenging situations for ourselves and others. So I like my creed to be explicit in some aspects of the way to unconditional Love of All.

Benefits

To navigate my life, I need to trust my decision-making ability. Much stress can be experienced through "second guessing" myself over past decisions. Even though my faith tells me God always gives me and my loved ones what we need, I still want to engage life as best I can to co-create that reality. When I have faith in my decision-making process, it supports my faith that the current situation is exactly as it should be. My faith brings me peace. It also makes decision-making in this moment more straightforward and less stressful.

The benefits of acceptance are huge. Judgments cause stress. They create and support unhelpful fears. Judgments against others keep us from developing close, supporting relationships with them. Our egos may say "good, I did not want anything to do with them anyway!" but when you have faith in Fundamental Unity, you know that is impossible. We are all related to each other and everything else, thank God!

Practicing radical acceptance supports humility. If we believe that all judgments against others are caused by ignorance and/or misunderstanding, then when we start to feel ourselves judging we can stop by admitting that we must not understand the situation deeply and clearly enough. How can I possibly understand all the factors that went into a person doing something that I judge to be "wrong" or "bad?" I can't, and luckily my faith does not require me even to make such an attempt. I need not understand everything, because I have faith that everyone and every situation is lovable exactly the way they are, even when they seem to be killing me! This is why Jesus taught us to Love our enemies. He understood the power of radical acceptance.

Creed Part 7: Spiritual Activism

"Raising my consciousness supports Love, peace and clarification of truth for others. This facilitates others' own process of raising consciousness, so manifest consciousness rises exponentially. my faith and practice supports this journey. i will live by this creed, updating it as I change and grow in Love. "

Because we are fundamentally unified and only superficially separate, our individual spiritual progress contributes to the Whole. For thousands of years, spiritual seekers have experienced this with the intellectual and energetic support of an enlightened teacher.[25]

---

[25] At the social level, this has been affirmed by the Transcendental Meditation (TM) Movement, which conducted a scientifically controlled study in Washington, DC in the summer of 1993. During the nearly eight weeks of the study, the meditation practice of 800-4,000 TM meditators effected a 23.3% drop in the predicted rate of violent crime in the city. http://www.worldpeacegroup.org/washington_crime_study.html, accessed 8/12/2017.

"Raising my consciousness supports Love, peace and clarification of truth for others. **This facilitates others' own process of raising consciousness, so manifest consciousness rises exponentially.** my faith and practice supports this journey. i will live by this creed, updating it as I change and grow in Love. "

In systems theory, any process that reinforces itself creates an exponential rate of change. For example, global warming is melting the ice at the earth's poles. Dark water absorbs more heat from the sun than white snow and ice, which increases the temperature of the water and air. The more it melts, the more the temperature goes up, which in turn increases the rate of melting, in a reinforcing cycle of accelerating change.

We live in an era of multiple threats to the survival of civilization. In order to solve the problems we have created, we need to see things differently. The problems can't be solved through the same paradigms that supported their creation. New belief systems are most readily adopted as consciousness rises, so raising human consciousness is a self-reinforcing process. In his book *Discovery of the Presence of God*, David Hawkins writes:

> With the addition of new information and the advancement of consciousness overall, the likelihood of reaching advanced states of consciousness is one thousand percent greater than before.

This is very encouraging: even as our world undergoes traumatic physical changes, our collective consciousness will continue to rise ever more rapidly. Hawkins spells this out quite clearly earlier in the same book:

> Each individual who transcends the levels of consciousness to their highest completion in this domain makes it easier for others to follow, just like the lead dog breaks the snow and facilitates the progress of the rest of the team. One's seeming individual spiritual endeavor serves all mankind. Each one who crosses over from below 200 to above 200 [on his scale of consciousness which I described earlier] has already enabled untold numbers to follow and serves as a potential instructor as well. One cannot become enlightened just for one's own self because the impact is felt throughout all of human consciousness. The spiritual seeker of today has the advantage that the consciousness level of all mankind is rising, and thus, there is less collective resistance.[26]

I'm glad we have at least this one trend of exponential change that reduces suffering!

> "Raising my consciousness supports Love, peace and clarification of truth for others. This facilitates others' own process of raising consciousness, so manifest consciousness rises exponentially. **my faith and practice supports**

---

[26] David R. Hawkins, Discovery of the Presence of God (Veritas Publishing, 2006), pp. 116 & 108, Kindle Edition loc. 1563 and 1463.

this journey. i will live by this creed, updating it as I change and grow in Love. "

I find it helpful to keep this bigger picture in my mind. This belief also stems from my most fundamental belief in Unity, but the ego is best subdued through reinforcing beliefs at many levels of understanding, so I find it useful to hold beliefs at multiple levels until they are no longer needed to support my practices. As this is the last part of my creed, it is lowest in the hierarchy I mentioned earlier and thus it is worded at a level of understanding that emphasizes separateness.

> "Raising my consciousness supports Love, peace and clarification of truth for others. This facilitates others' own process of raising consciousness, so manifest consciousness rises exponentially. my faith and practice supports this journey. **i will live by this creed, updating it as I change and grow in Love.** "

My beliefs are not set in stone. While I have found these beliefs very useful in recent years, I may well replace some with others in the future. (As we have learned in the Buddhist Diamond Sutra, all beliefs are like rafts that we use to cross a river, but that we must eventually abandon at the other shore in order to continue our journey.) In the meantime, I'll live by this creed to reap its many benefits, which fit the needs of my life quite well.

Benefits

I remember explaining to my mother, when I was a young adult, that one of my life-long goals was continuous self-development. I told her I wanted to continue to improve myself, be happier, by improving my various abilities. She wondered whether that might be selfish. I responded that by improving myself, I'd be better able to serve the world. Now my faith in Unity allows me to see all self-development as holistic and global. This belief reinforces the continuation of all my spiritual practices, since I understand that my own practices are helping others. In our culture that values "doing," this belief can be helpful to people who find it challenging to make time for meditation.

While sitting meditation, we tend to feel the pull to "do" the many things on our agendas. This distraction may keep us from sitting back down again tomorrow. But if we truly believe that raising our own consciousness is a beautiful and important gift to the world, it can help us reorganize our priorities. For me, this belief—that individual practice helps the world—inspires me to consider a monastic life, or at least to increase my attendance at extended practice retreats, especially at this critical time for our planet.

Believing that my meditation practice sessions benefit the world helps me to deepen my experience of Unity, even when I'm practicing by myself at home. This is self-reinforcing: the more experiences I've had of Unity the more I'm inspired to strengthen my practice.

This belief supports hope. In a world of so much uncertainty, with exponential growth factors driving technological, economic, environmental and social change at unprecedented and accelerating rates, my beliefs give me peace in the present moment and hope for our future. The belief in exponential growth of collective consciousness is the single most important cause of this hope.

As a spiritual activist committed to helping to reduce the suffering of others, my beliefs and spiritual practices are all I need to do my work. Unlike more traditional activists, I need not discern which of the many areas of world crisis to try to address, because raising consciousness supports the resolution and/or graceful understanding of all "problems."

5   Faithful Evolution

Spiritual life is like a journey across a beautiful and diverse landscape. Our beliefs are like the vehicles and tools we need, which must change throughout the journey. We need a rope to climb steep mountains and cliffs and a camel to cross a desert. When we come to a river, we build and use a raft, then abandon it on the other side because it is too heavy to carry (as taught by the Buddha). We don't need it on land, and we can always build another.

From one life to the next, and even during this one, our faith evolves. We may not always be aware of our faith-based beliefs or how they are subtly changing. Introspection allows us to determine our current beliefs, thus helping our faith evolve so it can support the life practices that will carry us through the current leg of our journeys.

Consciousness rises and falls throughout our lives, in small ways from moment to moment and, more dramatically, through longer periods of stress and contemplation. If a new belief is formed when we are experiencing higher consciousness, whether during an exceptionally moving worship service, on a mountain top, or during a meditation retreat, with spiritual will we can be led by that faith even when our consciousness sinks back down to lower levels. When faith-based beliefs come from a higher consciousness than what we normally experience, we are most fruitfully led by them. If, however, we allow beliefs that stem from lower consciousness to hold sway, then our lives can actually be held back by our faith. We can become rooted to our lowest consciousness, until those limiting beliefs are shaken and released. So it is very important to understand what we believe and how it is affecting our lives.

Faith in science helps guide some of our life choices. For example, we've learned that lead paint is poisonous and can cause brain damage, so when we move into an older house or apartment we ask if any of the paint contains lead, especially if we have young children. In most places the law requires disclosure of these kinds of hazards. We can't see the lead, so we trust scientifically developed testing methods to detect its presence. Similarly, we have faith in the science that led to laws banning the sale of lead paint.

Scientific evidence helps us make decisions about the physical world, but it falls short when it comes to relationships and actions that affect our neighbors.

When it comes to our loving relationships, belief in God in some form is a positive influence on our behavior. The form this motivation takes depends on how we experience and define God. Some believe that God is an all-powerful entity or being that passes judgment on us when we die to determine whether our souls will spend eternity in heaven or hell. The fear of hell can be a strong motivator to live a more loving life, but it comes at a high price when that fear is felt more than the anticipation of the reward of heaven. The energy and intention behind our actions is paramount to the quality of our lives, so motivations based on love are always preferable.

People who believe in a judgmental, vengeful God will have that belief reinforced whenever they experience pain and suffering. They will tend to think that God is punishing them for past transgressions or failures. Their faith is supported at fearful moments of lower consciousness. This reinforces the fear and creates more stressful situations in the future. Some spiral down and fall from grace altogether. They can't understand how God could allow such suffering. They can actually become atheists.

If we can learn to have more faith in heaven than we do in hell, our faith will be positively reinforced and we will move in the direction of grace and love. With enough practice, it becomes possible to believe in and experience God as perfectly loving, which eliminates the possibility of negative reinforcement.

What Do We Believe?

To consider changing our beliefs, we need to determine what we believe now and how that has been helping or hindering our life journey.

We don't have to believe in God in order to be led by faith. If we believe that the world is inherently good and beautiful, created through synergy, cooperation, and compassion, our belief will be positively reinforced in the high points of our lives. Our life's journeys will be enriched as a result.

We saw in Chapter 2 how some beliefs are reinforced in our low points, when we feel the pain and suffering of frustration, disappointment or anger. When we believe that our lives are governed by Murphy's Law, where the worst outcome is always assured, we must ask ourselves whether that has helped us continue our journey towards a more consistently happy, physically and emotionally healthy life?

To reflect on what we believe, we can review what we did and how we felt over the past week. Were there high or low points in our experience, and which of our strongest beliefs reinforced them? How often did we feel gratitude for what we had? When we took actions based on our beliefs, did they lead to increased happiness or suffering?

It is helpful to keep this self-evaluation process in mind to help better understand what we believe. Our beliefs are like skills, and we need to be aware of how they work. For example, when we ride a bike we are seldom aware of how it works. When we want to turn to the right, we are convinced we need to move the handlebars in that direction but, in reality, we must first turn them briefly to the left, causing the bike to lean to the right so it will bank around to make the turn. At times we steer our way through life using unconscious, poorly understood beliefs.

One way to uncover and explore what we believe now is to start from what we regularly spend time doing in our day-to-day lives. I've created a worksheet to facilitate this process, available as a free download from my website: http://www.oceanofspirit.org/faithtopractice/beliefworks heet.pdf The first page has two columns: the left for listing things we do and the right for beliefs that explain why we do them. The second page is designed to help us delve more deeply into one or more of our beliefs, by asking ourselves why we believe something. The goal of this process is to help us understand our faith-based, foundational beliefs.

Take as an example the person who often shovels an elderly neighbor's walk after snowstorms. The reason could be as simple as the good feeling he or she gets by knowing it is now possible for the neighbor to reach their mailbox the next day. Why does that feel good? If we carefully analyze the belief chain that leads us to this feeling, we will have the answer. We know how important it is to receive greeting cards in the holiday season, we see value in receiving these cards. We believe they help us stay connected to our loved ones. Why is that important? Because we believe that love based connections is what make life worth living. Why? Because we feel this belief in our hearts, it is part of our foundational faith. Every time we go to our own mailbox in the winter and receive a holiday card, the joy we feel is increased when we recall how we've helped our neighbor receive theirs. The gift of our time increases our ability to receive more gratefully It is a beautiful example of how we always receive through our giving, which we can only realize when we look deeply enough.

When using the worksheet, explore the activities that you spend the most time doing, as well as shorter ones that you do frequently, to see if they are supported by your most cherished and heartfelt beliefs.

For some of us it can be helpful to start a faith and practice journal, in which we note current beliefs as they are identified. Put each belief on the top of a new page, then list examples of how they support practices, actions and interpretations as they are discovered. Noting which beliefs we want to reinforce and those we want to release is especially helpful.

Taking the Next Step
in the Evolution of Our Belief System

Reviewing our faith and practice journals and completed belief worksheets to see which of our current beliefs we want to concentrate on changing or reinforcing is key to the evolution of our belief systems. The most important beliefs to evolve are the ones affecting the life practices and actions we are taking or would like to take.

For example, let's say we spend more money than we should on things we don't really need. There is probably a belief that supports this behavior, like "my happiness depends on the quality and quantity of my possessions." To work on releasing this belief, we can find, affirm and adopt an alternative one, which addresses that same area of your life, such as "I am very grateful that I already have more than enough things to be happy," or "my happiness stems from the love I bring to my personal relationships." When releasing one belief it is more effective to hold another in mind than it is to try to negate the thought we are releasing. The mind tends to manifest what we give it energy for, even if our intention is to release. When we find ourselves acting from and/or interpreting life through a belief we are releasing, we should gently remind ourselves of the new, alternative belief towards which we are moving.

Reviewing affirmations is a time-proven technique for self-improvement. We can write the belief we want to reinforce on a slip of paper and tape it to the bathroom mirror, where we will see it every morning and throughout our day. If we want to change our habits and beliefs about spending money, we can put it on a card in our wallet or purse.

It is helpful to distinguish between two kinds of faith: beliefs that we have solidly confirmed or realized through our own experience, and those we have not. By "confirmed" I mean something distinctly different from "proved." Proof is a line of reasoning, backed by evidence. Realization comes from within and requires no one else's agreement and therefore no reasoning. Note that this level of personal realization happens for people at all levels of consciousness, so even beliefs like "the world is out to get me," or "it takes hard work and sacrifice to build a good life for yourself," could be felt and "owned" at this level of personally integrated faith. All of us, regardless of our level of consciousness, need to constantly question our beliefs and be prepared to surrender them to God as we progress to realization of Divine union with our true being.

Beliefs that we have not yet fully realized as our own could be said to be the truly faith-based beliefs, because we not only can't prove them to anyone else, we have not even "proven" them to ourselves yet. We are trusting that what we have been taught by more spiritually advanced teachers is true, in order to stretch our beliefs through faith. This second type of "true faith" is a practice in its own right.

Examples of Evolution of My Faith

When I started practicing Transcendental Meditation (TM) at the age of 15, I was agnostic about the idea of "cosmic consciousness," as my teachers called it, or Enlightenment. It was the first I'd heard of the concept of raising consciousness through spiritual practices. I meditated twice daily to relieve stress, which I discovered was important to my mental health and happiness. This benefit, and many others, had been proven through scientific studies and I had a strong faith in science.

I attended Quaker Meeting in my 20s, where I started to believe in an all-loving God while practicing silence. I believe the energy of the people I was practicing silence with represented a higher level of consciousness than mine at the time, which helped me transition from being agnostic to understanding God as Love. Their loving intentions at Meeting for Worship allowed me to have a positive personal experience of the Divine. As I moved through life with this faith, it was affirmed during the most positive moments in my life, which were filled with comfort, love and joy.

When I was 46, I changed my middle name to Gaia. At the time I was changing my last name back to Kano from my married name of Munsey-Kano, so it seemed like a good opportunity to adopt a name that affirmed my current belief. Gaia refers to the theory that the Earth demonstrates traits of a single organism, and that the synergy between animals, plants, and elements resembles the cells and parts of our individual bodies. Earlier, I had been attracted to and adopted the belief that I was a small part of this whole. Though the theory had not been proven scientifically, I liked it enough to adopt it by faith. This belief was quite supportive of loving and kind choices, but is no longer one of my primary beliefs. In 2015 I realized that I'd become attached to the idea to such a degree that my ego was sometimes becoming planet sized. I had to release my attachment to this belief in order to continue my practices of radical acceptance and letting go of fears (see below).

I started to write this book in 2012, and am completing it in 2017. In those five years, my beliefs have shifted as I've continued my spiritual journey, providing evidence of how faith-based beliefs change and simplify as we continue to uncover our true Selves.

In 2015, my sister gave me, for my birthday, the book *I Am That: Talks with Sri Nisargadatta Maharaj*. I had originally put the book onto my wish list when I heard, in the movie documentary *With One Voice*,[27] what is perhaps his most famous quote: "When I realize I am nothing, that is wisdom. When I realize I am everything, that is Love. Between these two my life moves." That quote resonated with me deeply, so I promised myself I'd read more of Nisargadatta's teachings when I had a chance. Before he died in 1981, Nisargadatta held many conversations with seekers at his home in India. His main advice for spiritual practice was simply to stay with the sense "I am" as much

---

[27] With One Voice (2009), directed by Eric Temple.

of the day as possible. At the time I was interning for a year at Koinonia Farm and was already practicing mindfulness there, so this advice was fairly easy for me adopt. I silently thought the words "I am" at the end of every in and out breath, when the current activity allowed, which was most of the time. As an intern, I had few significant decisions to make and most of the work did not require that much thought once you got into it, so it was a very fruitful place to practice.

Even though I can never meet him face-to-face, I consider Nisargadatta to be my guru. I trust that his teachings and recommended practices will help me realize my true Self, to become enlightened. Since 2015 I've been studying his teachings most every night, usually just reading a few pages in bed just before I shut off the light. I have come to appreciate these teachings as very supportive of my existing practices, as described in this book. Through study and insight I've realized that the implications of the fundamental unity of All are far more profound than I had ever dared to imagine.

Nisargadatta's primary teachings, paraphrased, are:

I am not this human body. I am the ultimate source of all creation. I am primarily un-manifest awareness, witnessing each conscious being. Consciousness and manifestation appear spontaneously together, both are temporary and neither is fundamental to what I am. It is possible to become aware of consciousness itself, at a level of witnessing beyond consciousness.

Nisargadatta also teaches that there are no manifest causes, which is consistent with the teachings of Dr. David

Hawkins, whose books I've studied for many years and have referenced in this book. Both seem to be saying that everything springs from the un-manifest as a kind of package deal, and the idea that our actions are causing some of it to happen is an illusion. The way Nisargadatta most commonly describes this is through his adamant statement that the idea that you actually do anything is absolutely false, and that it's more accurate to say that things are done to you.

I have continued the practices I describe in this book, plus staying with the sense, "I am." I'm also doing my best to surrender all fears and desires, as Nisargadatta recommends. He teaches that only what is needed is "good" so all else is an illusory distraction from practice. I also do my best to take actions in life through faith in the beliefs he teaches, even though I have not realized them fully. I still do that by following my heart for the more significant decisions.

As a committed seeker of Enlightenment, everything that I do provides an opportunity for me to continue to practice "I am" and to try simply to witness what is happening and what I'm doing with no attachment to outcomes. By focusing on a mindful "I am" practice first and foremost, everything else can be done in a more relaxed and peaceful manner. I need not create any deadlines for myself, because whatever comes in each moment will always still be fine for practice. I have faith that my basic needs will always be met, as taught by Jesus in the Sermon on the Mount.[28]

---

[28] Matthew 6:25

While Nisargadatta did not mention these teachings often, he did address questions about the concept of destiny. He explained that destiny is of the container and name only, not the contents of the container. I interpret that to mean that the thoughts we choose to entertain and our intentions for our spiritual practices are up to us, while the physical manifestations of our lives are not controlled by the actions we seem to be choosing to take. I take the teachings he gave to each seeker with a grain of salt, because I believe that he automatically knew what beliefs and explanations were best for each listener, to support their spiritual practices. At this point I don't understand how destiny could be controlling our lives, but a belief in destiny does make it easier to practice in peace, playing the "game of manifest causes and their apparent effects" to meet my needs and leaving the rest to God.

One of the most important things Nisargadatta taught is that the beliefs we hold are less important than how we test them. Before I started to study his teachings I also had this insight, which was part of what inspired me to write this book. The spiritual practices we use to explore our beliefs are what matter most. Nisargadatta also emphasized the importance of being totally earnest in our practice, to have a strong desire to realize our true Selves, emphasizing that anything we intend to be a spiritual practice is one. Earnest intent combined with total devotion are what we need to uncover our goals. I experienced the truth of this teaching myself at Koinonia (as described in About the Author) when I experienced ubiquitous Love for All for the first time: I had fallen in love with the practice itself.

6   Responsible Happiness

Happiness is 95% interpretation and 5% circumstance. We must take care in what we believe! Dr. Richard J. Davidson says:

> We should really be thinking of happiness as a skill, which is no different from learning to play the violin, or learning to play golf.[29]

We want to *be* happy but in fact our culture teaches us we must *do* happy or *experience* happiness through our circumstances. This chapter discusses the art of being happy in its purest meaning.

Happy Beliefs

When we have sound faith foundations, we are in a good position to take responsibility for our happiness. A positive interpretation of our current situation will make it easier to act in ways that are consistent with our faith.

[29] Dr. Richard J. Davidson, speaking in the film Project Happiness (2011), directed by John Sorensen.

These interpretations and actions will help create future situations, for ourselves and others, that are even easier to see in a positive light.

There are many ways to practice our faith. Every moment is another opportunity to use our faith to nurture positive understandings that create inner peace and happiness.

For example, the other day I needed to get to the car rental office. My car had been rear-ended so it was in the shop and the insurance company had reserved a rental for me. I walked to the bus stop and boarded a red line bus waiting for its scheduled departure. The driver had stepped out to stretch his legs. When he came back and I told him where I was going, he told me I was on the wrong bus and the one I needed had just left. It would be two hours before I could get the next bus to my destination.

So I walked back home. It was a beautiful summer day and I decided to enjoy the extra walk back to my condo. After all, I had not been getting as much exercise as usual anyway, so I did not mind. When I got there I noticed my friend Al, sitting alone in the community gazebo, so I went to visit with him for a while.

I believe we create our own realities. I could have been angry at myself for not paying enough attention and boarding the wrong bus. I could have spent the entire walk back home thinking about the things I would have done with the time I had "wasted," but, given my faith, that would not have been the responsible interpretation of my situation. Because I believe that every situation is given to us for a reason, to provide an opportunity for us to grow in love, it was easy for me to remain grateful and happy. I fully enjoyed my extra walk and the chat with my neighbor.

Meditation, prayer, acts of loving kindness for a stranger, and finding ways to give of ourselves in every situation, are all examples of spiritual practices which nurture our abilities to respond in positive ways to any situation. We are literally practicing happiness, from within.

Happiness can never be sustained through increasing the quantity of anything, as our consumer culture would like us to believe. Instead, it stems from the quality of our experiences. It is the interpretation of our situation that matters. That is all. Most of us spend our lives making ourselves miserable through negative judgments of others and our circumstances. The most satisfying combination, to our ego selves, is to blame others or even the universe for our difficult situations. We want to deny responsibly for our misery, so we choose to be victims.

Master Our Minds

Thoughts deserve our attention, but many thoughts can be gently dismissed as unhelpful. If we find a sight disturbing, such as a dead animal on the side of the road, do we force ourselves to continue to look in that direction? Thoughts are like that. There is no need to beat ourselves up over a negative thought. We can allow ourselves to let go of that thought once we realize it is causing distress. When we have trouble doing that, we can do our best to just stay aware of the negative thought without giving it any additional energy. Once we know how, we can turn our awareness away towards something more constructive.

In the movie *With One Voice* the Hindu Sadhguru Jaggi Vasudev, Founder of the Isha Foundation, said, "Your mind is not taking instructions from you because you've never made an effort to understand how to operate this instrument. Any instrument that is out of control is more of a nuisance than of use."

Our minds are indeed troublesome organs. Too much of the average person's mind is occupied by thoughts that evoke, or are in response to, some form of fear. Worry, anxiety, anguish, disappointment, jealousy, regret are all too familiar to us. Yet most of us have received no training in the process of thought awareness, discernment, and release. Contemplative practices such as meditation, mindfulness, and silent prayer, help us to experience thoughts, or trains of thoughts, as discrete events. We can decide, through a practice of awareness, to reinforce and nurture the way we think of events or to gently release them to the universe.

Let me illustrate by using an example common to many of us:

Imagine we have a television in every room of our house. (Maybe we do). Then, imagine we have no control over their programming and they are always on. Furthermore, all the programming is about our personal lives!

In the kitchen, a TV announcer talks about future likely disasters that could happen any day. As you cook you hear, "Experts predict that your car will skid off the road in the next snowstorm. It will be totaled, and your insurance deductible is higher than your total savings so when you get that car fixed, you'll have to defer payments on important bills. Your cell phone won't work. It will be impossible for you to do your job and you'll get fired." The announcer continues to predict your eventual demise.

Now imagine that the TV in your living room is covering fears about your loved ones. "Your spouse is cheating on you, and you can't notice the signs" Or, "your children are using drugs and will eventually turn to a life of crime."

The TV in the bedroom reviews your past mistakes and their consequences, which you are currently struggling to tolerate. Vivid images of people you have hurt appear on the screen. Some are angry while others plan to take their revenge.

You really wish you could change the channels or at least have a room in the house where you could escape, but unfortunately the programming is ubiquitous and uncontrollable.

Our minds can be like this house: littered with unhelpful, fearful thoughts over which we have no choice or control. It's easy to see why many of us are unhappy much of the time. To shield ourselves from our unhappiness we seek entertainment and other experiences that will temporarily create positive, happy thoughts and feelings. We can actually be using our external lives to mask and distract us from our inner turmoil.

Buddhist masters teach that the mind is the sixth sensing organ. Thus, thoughts occur in our minds just as light and sound are sensed by our eyes and ears. The scientist Rupert Sheldrake has a hypothesis that our memories come from a connection to our past selves through time[30]. Research on that idea could lead to scientific proof of the ancient Buddhist teaching. But we don't have to know exactly how our minds experience thoughts to gain some control over the situation. We can practice meditation and mindfulness.

The many benefits of meditation are well-researched and documented, so I won't list them all here. Perhaps one of the most significant benefits is an opportunity to practice thought awareness. For example when we meditate through conscious breathing, we are taught to notice when our thoughts are taking us away from our breath and gently return to feeling it coming in and out of our body. Invariably thoughts occur many times over the course of a meditation session. That is good, because each time we "catch ourselves thinking" we are practicing this very important life skill. It hones the ability to become aware of and let go of a thought, until we get to the point where we automatically follow our trains of thought, allowing us to release unhelpful ones.

The conscious awareness from which we can discern thoughts is a mystical connection to God, the Universe, Universal Consciousness or whatever you want to call your Higher Power or concept of Unified being. What we call it does not matter. Self-awareness requires access to

---

[30] Rupert Sheldrake, Science Set Free (Deepak Chopra Books, 2006), p. 188.

this conscious awareness—the ocean on which the waves of thoughts flow.

Through mindfulness, we can practice accessing awareness while doing everyday tasks: washing the dishes, cooking, or raking the lawn, for example. First, we must silence the music or turn off the television. We can do our repetitive tasks mindfully, noticing our breathing, our simple motions and task experiences. We gently notice when our mind drifts to other thoughts, and go back to our task and our breathing. The fruit of this practice is the ability to choose our thoughts, so we can live happier lives.

Like any new skill, thought awareness takes some time to master. We may need to raise our consciousness (see Chapter 4, Creed part 4) before we can become more consistently successful at releasing unhelpful thoughts and feelings. We will need a strong faith in the benefits of meditation and other spiritual practices. We must choose our faith carefully, and we must review and revise it often, so it continues to support practices that improve our lives and strengthen our communities.

Finding Happiness in a Broken Heart

Variations in Love

In your despair
someone comforts you
helps you find some part of yourself to love
You love them for their gift of relief

Your anger overcomes you
until your savior rights some wrong
You love them for validating grievance
and for helping you find
a part of yourself
that you thought you lost

Bobbing in a sea of indifference
someone takes notice
You love them
because they love you for who you are

Heart broken
your love has left you for another
yet you love her still
more than she will ever know
Wanting only for her happiness

The perfect beauty of all things
radiates around you
You have no choice
but to Love perfection

Between thoughts
beyond feeling
no thing is needed
you Are Love

When I wrote this poem in 2012, I had experienced most
of these variations in Love, except for the last. As I
complete this book in 2017, I'm experiencing a version of
"being Love" much of the time. It is a strong and
wonderful feeling, which does not require a specific object
or experience. There are many more variations on the

feeling of love and, more importantly, an unlimited number of ways to give love. I'd like to share a personal story of Love, begun when I was a boy and continuing for many years.

When I was 12, I had my first consuming feelings of love for a girl. At least I thought I could love her. Sandy (I've changed her name for this telling) was a neighbor of ours on Cape Cod, where we spent our summers playing in and around the shores of Squeteague Harbor. Squeteague is an idyllic place for swimming and a popular mooring place for the boats we used for adventures in Buzzards Bay.

I spent the evenings then wandering the streets with my friends, chatting about tennis, sailing, the opposite sex, how we would get our next stash of beer, and other important things. The nights were warm and quiet. Sometimes we laid in the middle of the road to watch the stars.

My fondest memories are of the many evenings spent on the beach with Sandy. We would lie in silence for long periods, until one of us asked, "What are you thinking about?" I was usually thinking about how much I really wanted to roll onto my elbow and kiss her, but I was too shy, so I'd make up conversation and kill time until I could get up the nerve to make my move.

At that stage of my life journey, I had two main criteria for who I could love: someone I liked a lot, and someone who loved me. It did not occur to me that if both people had the same requirements for loving, it would be a stalemate: the condition of the other person loving first could never happen! Sixteen years later I would experience unconditional romantic love for the first time, but that is another story.

After my divorce in 2006, my thoughts of past flames increased and I imagined myself exploring a relationship with Sandy. She had not married, though I thought it likely she was in a serious relationship. We only saw each other a couple of times a year, so I was not sure. On one visit to the Cape, where she still lived, I gave her a copy of this poem:

First Love

We lay on the beach my love and I
Casting our thoughts into the sky
Solar systems and atoms are they one and the same?
Deep conversations were for me but a game

'Cause the context for me under each splendid sky
Were my feelings for you unrevealed, I was shy!
With attachment to outcome my love immature
I dared not risk losing, until I was sure

So my feelings lay silent, each and every long night
Until late in the summer my loss was in sight
Someone else had found you, affection was clear
Embraced near the fire, by another, my dear

Only then could I see what, attachment had wrought
Love tainted with fear, caused the loss that I sought
So I gathered my bag, my harp and my heart
Went alone to let go of what I never dared start

I released my attachment and let my love languish
Through good wishes for you I reduced my anguish
But somewhere deep down within my soul
My love for you has still remained whole

So as friend or as play mate, soul mate or lover
I know in my heart that I'll love you forever

I never mustered the nerve to tell Sandy how I felt that summer. I never asked for, or made my move to give her that first kiss, to see if it was welcome. As the summer wore on, even though we had many beautiful nights on the beach together, I had to admit that I would not dare to reveal my feelings before heading back to my winter home. It did not occur to me that my hesitation could lead to losing my chance.

Every summer, the day camp Sandy and I went to had an overnight trip to Bassett's Island. It would take multiple trips in the camp motor boat to ferry us across the narrow channel between the Scraggy Neck causeway and the nearest end of the island. When it started to get dark, we would make a fire on the beach and gather around it in our sleeping bags. We would tell ghost stories into the night and eat lots of candy.

Invariably one of the stories would describe the "green slime," a monster of the deep that ate small children when it had the chance. One of the counselors would always cover themselves with seaweed, sneak up to the fire while the tale was still being told, and at the perfect moment announce themselves with a threatening roar. Another counselor would scream "It's green slime!" The little kids and some of the older ones jumped up and ran away, while the counselors pretended to fight off the slime and drive it back into the water.

In the summer of my 12th year we stuck to all those traditions and I was having a wonderful time, even though I knew by then that the "green slime" was not real. After the commotion, I went for a little walk and on my return, there was Sandy snuggling with another boy. He was an older guy from Wild Harbor Yacht Club, whom we had met during a regatta. I was crushed.

I could not bear to rejoin the others by the fire. I took my sleeping bag and harmonica and walked to the other side of the island to be alone with my sorrow. There was a pretty strong wind, so I had to zip up my army surplus mummy bag to stay warm, as I improvised on the harmonica. I imagined the wind might even carry the sad sounds across the island to Sandy's ears, but I was kidding myself. She probably hadn't even noticed me leave the fire. I shed no tears, as I had not yet recovered from the standard, "big boys don't cry," teaching of the day, but my heart was broken.

I knew I cared about Sandy deeply, as a friend if nothing more. So I decided if she was happy, then I would be happy for her good fortune. I managed to find a happy response to the situation and felt much better in the morning.

Decades later, after she read the poem, she had no response. To this day I don't know what she thought about her old friend finally revealing his feelings of love. I suspect she never had romantic notions of me then or now, but at least she finally knew how I felt.

7   Summary and Conclusion

When I first wrote on this subject, it was for a short reflections presentation for the mid-day chapel service at Dartmouth College. The title of my "mini sermon" was "Faith Foundations."[31]

That was back in 2007. The main point of that reflection was that all our beliefs rest on a foundation of faith, even when those foundational beliefs are what some people call "common sense" assumptions.

As I write this summary, it is 2017. In the years between that first presentation and now, my faith has evolved, as I briefly shared in Chapter 5, Faithful Evolution. Certainly the emphasis I place on each facet of my faith has shifted, although faith in fundamental Unity is still most important to me. By my own intended practice, it would be time to update my creed, but one of the beliefs that I've depreciated a bit over the years is the importance to codify things as they change. As long as my

---

[31] The original text is available online:
http://oceanofspirit.org/davidgaiakano/?p=210

beliefs continue to support my spiritual practices, they are doing their "job." As a full time contemplative, I now measure my practice in terms of quality. How consistently am I able to stay with the sense "I am"? How do my life decisions support this continuous practice? My process is now grounded in the faith that reaching Enlightenment is the most worthy goal, along with helping others to raise their own consciousness.

I hope the ideas in this book have inspired you, the reader, to work toward understanding your current beliefs, and living more fully by the life-supporting ones that you want to keep. I also hope that you have already started to explore faith-based beliefs that are newer to you, that will better support practices that you want to start or strengthen. Most of us grow and change throughout our lives and as we do, our beliefs and routine practices need updating too.

As we deepen our faith exploration, we are bound to hear beliefs that seem "far out" to us, such as the fundamental Unity of everything, or that everyone is lovable, even the cruelest murderer. We may not yet be ready to adopt certain beliefs, or certain interpretations of our religious tradition's teachings. Just as we must abandon a raft (of belief) once we reach the other shore, there is no need to carry an unneeded raft before we reach the river. If we remain flexible and open, we can build ourselves new faith-based beliefs as we need them. It doesn't matter so much what we believe; it's how we test, or practice through those beliefs, that counts. The important thing is for our faith-based beliefs to support practices that keep us moving on our journey.

In this book I've mentioned personal practices that may not seem spiritual, like spending quality time with our loved ones. Anything is a spiritual practice if we intend it that way, but even then, some may be more fruitful than others. Although my own focus is on spiritual practice, those who don't identify themselves as particularly spiritual can benefit from this book too. If you are one of those readers, I hope this book has helped you identify and/or strengthen wholesome life practices to make them a more regular part of your routine.

The best way for us to reach any wholesome goal is through regular spiritual practices that help to raise our consciousness. Over the years my belief in the importance of consciousness to every aspect of life has only strengthened. I'd like to leave you with some examples of how that works, which I've experienced in my own life.

We sometimes feel down and out, and wonder why. Raising our consciousness will not only illuminate our emotional quandaries, but resolve them too.

We can heal ourselves by releasing unhelpful thoughts and feelings, which gets easier the longer we hold that intention. We can surrender them through the practices of current-moment mindfulness and acceptance. We can literally practice happiness as we raise our consciousness.

We sometimes wonder why we have so much trouble creating and staying in healthy relationships. Raising our consciousness will not only help us better understand ourselves and loved ones, but it will actually make us more attractive to mates who are healthier for us.

We worry that our loved ones are making choices that could result in suffering. Raising our consciousness will show us that the most helpful thing we can do is to model good choices. We must trust that every aspect of their lives, even the most painful, are opportunities for them to learn and grow.

We sometimes feel helpless when we see our world floundering. Raising our consciousness automatically helps everyone, and requires convincing ourselves alone to take the needed actions. I call this spiritual activism. The enlightened gurus teach that every manifest thing springs from un-manifest causes. Raising our consciousness is the only way to make a real contribution to our world.

Spiritual practice is a group activity. Often the key to success in a lifetime of practice is just physically showing up to practicing meditation, prayer, yoga, worship and so on with one or more spiritual communities. As the Buddha said, the three elements we need are the Buddha (Universal being), the Dharma (teachings), and the Sangha (community of practice). Christ said, "For where two or three gather in my name, there am I with them."[32] I hope this book has inspired you to spend more time with your community of faith, or seek out a new group if you have none. A group that resonates with you can help you to live more fully through your faith.

Finally, I hope that this book has fostered self-love, regardless of where you are in your journey. We have all held unhelpful beliefs that we needed to shed in order to move forward. We have all been impatient with ourselves

---

[32] Matthew 18:20.

and those around us. We have all felt shame, anger, jealousy and other fear-based emotions. When we have faith to enter a path of wholesome practice, we can learn from our flaws by noticing how they are distracting us from our true selves. We can learn to love ourselves as we are now, so that we can fully embrace the practices that are raising our consciousness, for the benefit of All.

Poem Index

CPSIA information can be obtained
at www.ICGtesting.com
Printed in the USA
BVHW031816071118
532446BV00001B/52/P

9 781976 274299